NUTSHELLS

TRUSTS
IN A NUTSHELL

Other Titles in the Series

AUSTRALIA
LBC Information Services
Sydney

CANADA
Carswell
Toronto ● Ontario

NEW ZEALAND
Brookers
Auckland

SINGAPORE AND MALAYSIA
Thomson Information (S.E.) Asia
Singapore

This book is dedicated to Rupert Sydenham who used, and made filial comments on, the second edition, and did most of the work for the third.

The author also acknowledges with thanks the help received, for the first and second editions, from Dr. Geoff Gilbert, LL.B., LL.M. (Virg.) Barrister and Senior Lecturer in Law, University of Essex.

NUTSHELLS

TRUSTS
IN A NUTSHELL

FOURTH EDITION

by

Angela Sydenham, M.A., LL.B. (Cantab.)
Solicitor, Birketts, Ipswich

London ● Sweet & Maxwell ● 1997

First Edition 1987
Reprinted 1988
Reprinted 1990
Second Edition 1991
Third Edition 1994
Reprinted 1996
Fourth Edition 1997

Published by Sweet & Maxwell Limited of
100 Avenue Road, Swiss Cottage, London, NW3 3PF
Phototypeset by
Wyvern Typesetting Limited, Bristol
Printed in England by Clays Ltd, St Ives plc

A CIP catalogue record
for this book is available
from the British Library

ISBN 0-421-588705

CONTENTS

1. DEFINITIONS AND CLASSIFICATIONS OF TRUSTS

DEFINITIONS

Various textbook writers have attempted definitions of a trust. Professor Keeton gave the following:

> "A trust ... is the relationship which arises wherever a person called the trustee is compelled in equity to hold property, whether real or personal, and whether by legal or equitable title, for the benefit of some persons (of whom he may be one and who are termed beneficiaries) or for some object permitted by law, in such a way that the real benefit of the property accrues, not to the trustee, but to the beneficiaries or other objects of the trust."

Not a very easy definition to remember. The essential characteristic is the split between the management of the property which is vested in the trustees and the beneficial interest of the property which is in the beneficiaries. Sometimes the trustees and the beneficiaries are the same people.

Trusts distinguished from other legal concepts

1. Contracts. There are many differences between a contract and a trust.
(a) Contracts are an invention of common law, trusts of equity.
(b) Contracts generally create only a personal right, trusts a right in the property itself, a right *in rem*.
(c) Contracts are enforceable only if supported by consideration or made in a deed; a beneficiary under a properly constituted trust can enforce the trust even where he has not given any consideration.
(d) Contracts cannot usually be enforced by third parties, a rule which is subject to limited statutory exceptions (*e.g.* Law of Property Act 1925, s.56 as restrictively interpreted, and the Married Women's Property Act 1882, s.11). A beneficiary can enforce a trust where he or she is not a party to the agreement between the settlor and the trustees.

One very important consequence of an arrangement being a trust, as opposed to a contract, arises on the insolvency of the person in whom the property is vested. If a beneficiary can establish a trust the trust property will not be available to the trustees' creditors. Where no such trust can be established anyone entitled to the property will be able to claim only with the other unsecured creditors. Sometimes an arrangement will amount to both a contract and a trust.

In *Barclays Bank Ltd v. Quistclose Investments Ltd* (H.L., 1970) Rolls Razor Ltd declared dividends on shares which it could not pay. Quistclose agreed to make a loan for the purpose of paying the dividends. The money was paid into a special account at Barclays Bank. Rolls then went into liquidation, with a large overdraft at Barclays. The bank claimed they were entitled to the money in the special account to reduce the overdraft. The House of Lords held that Quistclose had paid the money for a particular purpose. On the failure of that purpose the bank held the money on a resulting trust for Quistclose. The bank was not entitled. The fact that there was a contract for a loan from Quistclose did not exclude the implication of a trust. This case was followed in *Carreras Rothmans Ltd v. Freeman Mathews Treasure Ltd* (1984) and *Re EVTR Ltd* (1987).

The recipient may decide to treat money received as impressed with a trust rather than merely a contractual prepayment. In *Re Kayford Ltd (In Liquidation)* (1975) a mail order company opened a special bank account for money received from customers. This money was not available to the liquidator when the company was subsequently wound up.

2. Powers. The difference between powers and trusts are:

(a) Powers can be legal. A power of attorney, for instance, can authorise the conveyance of a legal estate. They can also be equitable. In the case of powers of appointment they can only be equitable. Trusts are always equitable.

(b) A power is discretionary. A trust imposes a duty. Thus if a trustee does not carry out his or her duties the court will intervene. The court will not intervene to compel a person to exercise a power.

(c) A potential beneficiary under a power has no interest in the property before it is appointed to him or her unlike a beneficiary of a trust. If all the beneficiaries of a trust, being absolutely entitled and of full age and *sui juris*, agree, they can terminate the trust, *Saunders v. Vautier* (1841). And this still applies where they are objects only of a discretionary trust.

(d) The rule of certainty of objects used to be different for powers and trusts. Trustees would need a full list of beneficiaries before they could carry out their duties. This was unnecessary where someone had only a power. It was sufficient if it could be said of any given individual that he or she was or was not within the class of objects specified by the donor of the power. Since *McPhail v. Doulton* (H.L., 1971) the rule for powers has been extended to discretionary trusts. The old rule remains for fixed trusts.

(e) If a donee of a power makes no appointments the property reverts to the settlor or his estate. If there is a discretionary trust and no appointments are made the beneficiaries take equally.

It is often very difficult to decide whether there is a trust with a power of selection or a mere power. In *Burroughs v. Philcox* (1840) the testator gave property to his two children for their lives, and gave the survivor of them power to dispose of the property by will "amongst my nephews and nieces or their children, either all to one of them, or to as many of them as my surviving child should think proper." It was held that a trust was created in favour of the testator's nephews and nieces subject to a power of selection. As the surviving child had failed to exercise the power the property was divided equally amongst the objects.

A mere power rather than a trust with a power of appointment will exist where there is a gift over in default of any appointment in favour of the objects, *Re Mills* (1930). If there is not a gift over then the settlor may or may not have created a trust. It will be a trust where he or she has shown an intention that the property shall in any event go to the beneficiaries.

In *Re Weeks's Settlement* (1897) a wife left property to her husband with a power "to dispose of all such property by will amongst our children." The court held there was no intention to create a trust even though there was no gift over.

3. Administration of a deceased's estate. Trusts were originally enforced by the Chancellor. The administration of the estate of a deceased person was under the control of the Ecclesiastical Courts. In many ways the duties of trustees, administrators and executors are similar and most of the provisions of the Trustees Act 1925 apply to all three, as does Part I of the Trusts of Land and Appointment of Trustees Act 1996.

Where a testator leaves a will appointing executors they will usually obtain a grant of probate from the Probate Registry. Although their powers relate back to the testator's death their ability to deal with the assets of the deceased is often limited until they can produce the grant showing their legal entitlement. Where the deceased has left no will administrators will be appointed by the Probate Registry to deal with the estate. Their powers come from being granted letters of administration.

Distinctions between trusts and administration include the following:

(a) The job of executors and administrators, both often referred to as personal representatives, is to wind up and distribute the deceased's estate. The job of trustees is to hold property on behalf of the beneficiaries.

(b) Until the personal representatives assent to the property vesting in those entitled under the will or intestacy, or in a purchaser, they hold both the legal and beneficial interest in the property. In a trust the beneficiaries have the beneficial interest in the property.

(c) Under the Limitation Act 1980 claims to the personal estate of the deceased are statute-barred after 12 years. A beneficiary only has six years to claim against a trustee for breach of trust. Neither time limit applies where there has been fraud or where the personal representative or trustee retains the property or has converted it to his own use.

(d) One of several personal representatives can dispose of personal property. Trustees must always act jointly.

(e) A personal representative holds land on trust. When he sells the land he can give a good receipt for capital money without having to appoint another trustee (L.P.A. 1925, s.27(2)). Where trustees hold land on trust, or a tenant for life has the land vested in him under a strict settlement, two trustees are necessary to give a good receipt.

(f) Personal representatives can be appointed only by the will or by the court. New trustees however can be appointed by persons specified in the trust instrument or given that power under the Trustee Act 1925, or following a direction given by beneficiaries under the Trusts of Land and Appointment of Trustees Act 1996.

When the administration of an estate is completed the executors may have duties as trustees conferred on them by the will. Where there is an intestacy administrators are constituted express trustees (Administration of Estates Act 1925, s.33(1), s.46(1)). It is often difficult to tell when personal representatives change their capacity and become trustees. In the case of land a written assent is necessary to vest the legal estate in them as trustees. Until this is done the personal representative cannot appoint a new trustee, *Re King's W.T.* (1964). An implied assent is sufficient for personal property.

CLASSIFICATION OF TRUSTS

Trusts are classified in different ways by different writers. There is no general agreement on what is the proper classification.

1. Express trusts. These are trusts created by an express declaration or by a transfer to trustees on express trusts.

2. Implied trusts. This term may refer to resulting trusts, some kinds of constructive trusts and mutual wills, and trusts imposed by statute.

3. Resulting trusts. These arise where the beneficial interest "results" back to the settlor or his estate.

4. Constructive trusts. These are trusts which are imposed irrespective of intention, where it would be unjust for the holder of the property to hold it for his own benefit.

5. Private trusts. These are trusts for the benefit of an individual or class. They are enforceable by beneficiaries.

6. Public trusts. These trusts are charitable and enforceable by the Attorney-General.

7. Trusts of imperfect obligation. These are trusts for purposes other than charitable purposes. They are generally unenforceable.

8. Executed and executory trusts. An executed trust arises where all the details have been worked out. An executory trust is a valid trust but a further document is necessary to carry into effect the settlor's full intentions.

9. Completely and incompletely constituted trusts. Unless there is a declaration of trust or the trust property is vested in trustees it is not a completely constituted trust. Incompletely constituted trusts are not enforceable by volunteers.

10. Trusts of real property.   These may take two forms.

(a) Strict settlement. The legal estate is vested in the tenant for
life who is a trustee of his powers whereas the trustees of the
settlement have general supervisory powers over the settlement. The main duty of the trustees is to receive capital
money. Strict settlements apply only to land. New strict
settlements cannot be created after the commencement of
the Trusts of Land and Appointment of Trustees Act 1996.

(b) Trusts of Land. All trusts involving land, including mixed
trusts of land and personalty, but excluding existing strict
settlements, become trusts of land under the Trusts of Land
and Appointment of Trustees Act 1996. Trusts of land,
whether express, implied, resulting or constructive, include
trusts for sale and bare trusts. The legal estate is vested in
the trustees who have power to sell the land and overreach
the interests of the beneficiaries.

   Where statutory provisions formerly implied a trust for
sale there is now a trust of land without a duty to sell. An
express trust of land may or may not contain a duty to sell.
Notwithstanding any agreement to the contrary there will
always be a power to postpone the sale.

11. Illegal trusts.   Trusts will not be enforceable if they offend:

(a) against morality or public policy, *e.g.* a trust to seal up a house
for 20 years, *Brown v. Burdett* 1882; or

(b) the provisions of any statute; or

(c) the law of perpetuities. This is concerned with the vesting of
property at too remote a time in the future and the tying up
of capital or the accumulation of income for too long a period.

12. Illusory trusts.   These are trusts where a debtor transfers
property to a trustee for his creditors. These can sometimes be
revoked on the ground that they are not real trusts but merely an
arrangement made by the debtor for his personal convenience in
paying off his debts. The trusts cannot be revoked where:

(a) the creditors execute the deed; or

(b) the deed is communicated to the creditors who act upon it; or

(c) the trust is to arise only after the debtor's death; or

(d) there is an intention to create a proper trust.

2. CERTAINTIES

In order to have a valid trust there must be:
  (a) Certainty of words or intention.
  (b) Certainty of subject-matter.
  (c) Certainty of objects.

These requirements were specified by Lord Langdale M.R. in *Knight v. Knight* (1840).

CERTAINTY OF WORDS OR INTENTION

Certainty of words means that the settlor has shown an intention to create a trust. The word "trust" itself does not have to be used, as long as the words used show that intention. Sometimes it may be difficult to establish. In the older cases even precatory words, those words which express a hope or desire that the donee will hold the gift for another, have sometimes been sufficient to create a trust. By the end of the nineteenth century the attitude of the courts had changed.

In *Lambe v. Eames* (1871) the testator gave his estate to his widow "to be at her disposal in any way she thinks best for the benefit of herself and her family." It was held that this did not create a trust and she took absolutely. A similar decision was reached in *Re Adams and The Kensington Vestry* (1884) where the gift was "unto the absolute use of my dear wife in full confidence that she will do what is right as to the disposal thereof between my children either in her lifetime or by will after her decease."

In *Comiskey v. Bowring-Handbury* (1905), the House of Lords held that in looking for certainty of words or intention one should construe the document as a whole. In that case, a majority held that a testamentary gift to the widow "in full confidence" that having made such use of it as he would have made himself she would divide it amongst their surviving nieces was sufficient to create a trust in favour of the nieces.

The modern tendency is to hold that there is no trust, but the testator is merely saying what he would like to happen or is explaining the motive for the gift. If, however, the testator has used a precedent which would have created a trust under the old cases, that may be an indication that he intended to create a trust, *Re Steele's Will Trusts* (1948). Also a trust may be found even where there is no document. In *Paul v. Constance* (1977) there was held to be a trust where a bank account was opened in the name of Mr. Constance but an arrangement was made that his mistress could draw on the account. The surrounding facts indicated an intention that she was to have a beneficial share in the account.

Where there is no certainty of intention the person entitled to the property will take absolutely.

CERTAINTY OF SUBJECT-MATTER

Trust property

The trust property, the subject-matter of the trust, must be certain. Thus a declaration concerning the "bulk of my estate" will be ineffective to create a trust, *Palmer v. Simmonds* (1854). However, a trust of a specified number of shares, of one class in one company, even though there was no identification of the particular shares within the class, was held not to be void for lack of certainty as to subject matter *Hunter v. Moss* (1994).

Where there is no certainty of trust property, there can be no trust. The property, whatever it is, will remain with the settlor or if he is dead will either form part of his residuary estate or pass according to the rules of intestacy.

Beneficial interest

The size of the beneficial interest to be taken by each person must be certain. If it is not then the result will be the same as on failure of the trust property unless:

(a) it is a discretionary trust. The beneficial interest will not be deemed uncertain where trustees are given power to allocate the property amongst the beneficiaries as the trustees see fit; or

(b) the court can apply the maxim "equality is equity" and so divide the gift equally between the beneficiaries; or

(c) the main gift is to one beneficiary, subject to the rights of other beneficiaries to an undefined portion of the property. In that case only the undefined portion fails with the result that the one beneficiary takes the entire gift.

This is illustrated by *Sprange v. Barnard* (1789) where there was a gift to Thomas Sprange with a provision that at his death "the remaining part of what is left that he does not want for his own wants and uses" should go to the testator's brother and sister. It was held that Sprange was absolutely entitled to the whole gift. In another case *Curtis v. Rippon* (1820) the testator gave property to his wife "trusting that she will, in fear of God and in love to the children committed to her care, make such use of it as shall be for her own and their spiritual and temporal good, remembering always, according to circumstances, the Church of God and the poor." This was hopelessly vague as far as the amounts for the church and poor were concerned. The widow took all the property absolutely.

CERTAINTY OF OBJECTS

The objects, or beneficiaries of a trust, must be certain. If they are not but the other two certainties are present, there will be a resulting trust for the settlor or his estate.

Much confusion is caused in this topic by inconsistent use of terminology by textbook writers and judges. Conceptual uncertainty means uncertainty in the definition of the class which is to benefit. "First cousins" is certain, "those who have helped me" is uncertain. Evidential uncertainty is the evidence a particular claimant must prove if he is to come within the class. If it cannot be proved of a particular person that he is within the specified class or that he is outside the class, this will probably indicate that the class is *conceptually* uncertain.

A trust will never fail for lack of ascertainability, that is as to the whereabouts or continued existence of the beneficiary. The money can be paid into court and steps taken to trace the beneficiary.

Background

The rules governing certainty of objects used to be different for trusts and powers. In the case of a trust, the duty of trustees used to be to consider the claims of all possible beneficiaries. If they failed to do so the court would intervene and administer the trust by an equal division of the fund. The trustees would therefore need to have a complete list of the beneficiaries. Today where there are discretionary trusts, not just for families but for large groups of people such as employees and dependants, a complete list is a practical impossibility and it has been realised that an equal division is inappropriate.

Those having a power of appointment are not under a duty to exercise the power. In the absence of *mala fides*, the court will not intervene to force them to do so. There has never therefore been the same rationale for having a complete list of potential beneficiaries of a power.

1. Fixed trust. A fixed trust is where the interest of the beneficiaries is specified in the trust instrument. It may be a trust for persons successively, to A for life with remainder to B or for persons concurrently, "to all my children in equal shares." In order to administer the trust the trustees must have a complete list of the beneficiaries at the time of distribution.

2. Powers. "A power is valid if it can be said with certainty whether any given individual is or is not a member of the class and does not fail simply because it is impossible to ascertain every member of the class." This, according to Lord Wilberforce in *McPhail v. Doulton* (H.L., 1971) is the effect of the House of Lords decision in *Re Gulbenkian's Settlement Trusts* (1970). The House of Lords in *Gulbenkian* rejected *obiter* the view that a power was valid if any *one* person clearly fell within the scope of the power even if there was doubt about the others.

A power will not be uncertain if the trustees are able to add to the class of beneficiaries, but a power could be invalid if it were capricious, *Re Manisty's Settlement* (1974) where Templeman J. said "a power to benefit 'residents of Greater London' is capricious because the terms of the power negative any sensible intention on the part of the settlor."

The courts are not concerned with whether or not a power is administratively unworkable. This is because the court cannot intervene where trustees choose not to exercise their power (*cf. Mettoy Pension Trustees Ltd v. Evans* (1991) where the court did intervene to protect beneficiaries of a pension fund trust. The employer had a fiduciary power to use any surplus funds to benefit the employees or itself. The employer was insolvent and the court held that the money should go to the employees rather than the creditors).

3. Discretionary trust. A discretionary trust is where a discretion is given to trustees to select amongst a class of beneficiaries. Since *McPhail v. Doulton* (H.L., 1971) the rule for certainty of objects for discretionary trusts is the same as for powers.

In that case there was a trust to provide benefits for the staff of Matthew Hall & Co. Ltd, their relatives and dependants. The wording in the trust deed was "The trustees shall apply the net income of the fund in making at their absolute discretion grants to or for the benefit of any of the officers and employees or ex-officers or ex-employees of the company or to any relatives or dependants of any such persons in such amounts at such times and on such conditions (if any) as they think fit." The House of Lords held that it was not necessary to have a complete list. The test was "can it be said with certainty that any given individual is or is not a member of the class." The case was then referred to the Chancery Division and later to the Court of Appeal to decide if this test was satisfied.

In these later proceedings the case was heard under the name *Re Baden (No. 2)* (1973), Baden being the author of the trust. The Court of Appeal decided that the test was satisfied but there was a divergence of judicial reasoning. Stamp L.J. considered that the court must be able to say of any person that he is or is not a member of the class. If the question could not be answered then the trust was void.

To quote his words:

> "validity or invalidity is to depend on whether you can say of any individual—and the accent must be on that word 'any' for it is not simply the individual whose claim you are considering who is spoken of—that he is or is not a member of the class for only thus can you make a survey of the range of objects or possible beneficiaries."

This looks very like a return to the list principle, for one interpretation of these words is that it must be possible to say of *every* potential member of the class that he is or is *not* within the class. The difficulty will often arise in proving a negative.

On the facts of *Baden* it would have been impossible to establish that someone was not a relative in the sense of being descended from a common ancestor. Stamp L.J. avoided this conclusion by taking relative to mean next-of-kin. Sachs L.J. took the view that anyone not proved to be within the class was clearly outside it so that there was no room for a "don't know" category. Megaw L.J. held that as long as the court could say of a substantial number that they were or were not within the class it did not matter that there were some "don't knows." Even where there is certainty, the class may be so wide as to be administratively unworkable, *Re Hay's Settlement Trusts* (1981).

In *R. v. District Auditor No. 3 Audit District of West Yorkshire Metropolitan County Council, ex p. West Yorkshire MCC* (1986) a gift was held administratively unworkable, even though it was not capricious, where the councillors had voted to set up a trust to benefit the 2.5 million inhabitants of West Yorkshire.

4. Individual gifts to persons answering a particular description. Where there is a condition precedent attached to a series of individual gifts, it does not matter if it is uncertain if some individuals can satisfy the condition. The size of the gift to any person who does qualify will not be altered by the numbers in the class. In *Re Barlow's Will Trusts* (1979) the testatrix directed her executor to allow any of her friends who wished to do so to purchase her paintings at a price below the market value. The direction was held sufficiently certain. As long as one person qualified as a friend it did not matter about any uncertainty concerning the others.

Summary of Rules on Certainties

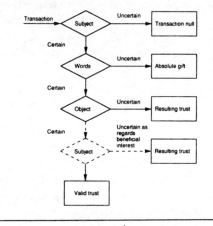

3. FORMALITIES

DECLARATION OF TRUST

1. Section 53(1)(b) of the Law of Property Act 1925 provides:

> "a declaration of trust respecting any land or any interest therein must be manifested and proved by some writing signed by some person who is able to declare such a trust or by his will."

The section does not apply to:
(a) resulting, implied or constructive trusts (L.P.A. 1925, s.53(2));
(b) trusts of personal property, which therefore may be declared orally. *Paul v. Constance* (1977).

The trust does not have to be declared in writing, only proved by some writing. The writing can come into existence after the trust has been declared but must contain all the terms of the trust, *Smith v. Matthew* (1861).

2. Trusts created by will. These take effect only on the death of the testator and must comply with section 9 of the Wills Act 1837 as amended by section 17 of the Administration of Justice Act 1982:

"No will shall be valid unless:
  (a) it is in writing, and signed by the testator or by some other person in his presence and by his direction; and
  (b) it appears that the testator intended by his signature to give effect to the will; and
  (c) the signature is made or acknowledged by the testator in the presence of two or more witnesses present at the same time; and
  (d) each witness either—
      (i) attests and signs the will; or
      (ii) acknowledges his signature in the presence of the testator (but not necessarily in the presence of any other witness),
but no form of attestation shall be necessary."

DISPOSITIONS OF INTEREST UNDER A TRUST

Section 53(1)(c) of the Law of Property Act 1925 provides:

"a disposition of an equitable interest or trust subsisting at the time of the disposition, must be in writing signed by the person disposing of the same or by his agent thereunto lawfully authorised in writing or by will."

The section applies to all property; personal property as well as land, although section 53(2) provides that section 53(1) does not apply to resulting, implied or constructive trusts.

The disposition has to be made not merely evidenced in writing, *cf.* L.P.A. 1925, s.53(1)(b).

Some specific examples of the operation of sections 53(1)(b) and (c)

Often it is not clear whether a transaction amounts to a declaration of trust or a disposition of an equitable interest. The cases are inconsistent and illogical. This is because many of them are revenue cases. The Revenue is anxious to find a disposition rather than a declaration because dispositions have to be in writing and writing attracts stamp duty while oral arrangements do not. Stamp duty is charged on an instrument rather than on the transaction itself. (Since the Finance Act 1985 stamp duty on gifts has been abolished.) In the *Vandervell* cases (see below) it was in the interest of the Revenue to establish for surtax reasons that there had been a disposition which was ineffective for lack of writing.

The following principles arise from the cases:
  (a) On an assignment of an equitable interest, two documents

can be read together, *Re Danish Bacon Co. Ltd Staff Pension Fund Trust* (1971). In that case an employee nominated his wife to receive benefits under a pension scheme should he die before he was entitled. He signed the approved form. Later he changed the nominated beneficiary by a letter. Megarry J. was doubtful whether the nomination was an assignment of a subsisting equitable interest within section 53(1)(c) but held that even if it was, the two documents could together constitute the necessary writing.

(b) A direction to trustees to hold on trust for another comes within section 53(1)(c) and so must be in writing. In *Grey v. I.R.C.* (H.L., 1960) a settlor made six settlements of nominal sums in favour of his grandchildren. Subsequently he transferred shares to trustees to hold on a bare trust for himself. He then orally directed the trustees to hold those shares on the trusts of the grandchildren's settlements. The trustees executed documents confirming they held the shares on the trusts of the settlements. The House of Lords held that the confirmation of the new trusts by the trustees was, in effect, a disposition within section 53(1)(c) by the beneficiary under the bare trust, Mr Grey. It transferred the equitable interest from the settlor to the beneficiaries of the settlements. Thus the oral direction was ineffective. The documents which the trustees executed therefore were not merely confirmatory but effected the disposition. *Ad valorem* stamp duty was payable on such documents.

(c) An oral direction by a beneficiary to trustees holding on a bare trust for him to transfer the legal as well as the equitable interest to a third party will be effective. The formal transfer of the legal ownership will automatically carry with it the equitable interest without a separate disposition of that interest. In *Vandervell v. I.R.C.* (H.L., 1967) the National Provincial Bank was holding shares on a bare trust for Vandervell. He directed the bank to transfer the shares to the Royal College of Surgeons subject to an option to repurchase which was given to the Vandervell trustees. An argument by the Revenue that he needed a document to transfer the equitable interest in the shares failed. The Revenue, however, succeeded in establishing that Vandervell still had an interest in the option. Although the option was validly vested in the Vandervell trustees, as the terms of the trusts had not been spelt out, there was a resulting trust to Vandervell of the benefit of the option.

(d) A declaration of trust by *trustees* with the consent of the beneficial owner will be treated as a valid declaration even if made orally, for it is not within the ambit of section 53(1)(c). To continue with the Vandervell saga, in 1961 Vandervell instructed his trustees to exercise the option given to them. The trustees used £5,000 from a trust for Vandervell's children. The Revenue claimed that Vandervell had not disposed of his equitable interest in the shares. In 1965 Vandervell executed a document by which he transferred any interest he had in the shares to the trustees to hold on trust for the children. This satisfied the Revenue whose claim was therefore limited to the period from 1961, the date of the exercise of the option, to 1965, the date of the deed. Meanwhile Vandervell had died and his executors claimed that his estate, rather than the Vandervell trustees, were entitled to the dividends on the shares between 1961 and 1965. *Re Vandervell Trusts (No. 2)* (1973) was brought by the executors. The Court of Appeal held that there was a valid declaration of trust by the trustees in 1961 when they exercised the option and this had the effect of terminating the resulting trust in favour of Vandervell. Vandervell's executors were not therefore entitled to the dividends. Consequently the Revenue's claim for surtax from 1961–1965 also failed. This case has been heavily criticised. It is difficult on the facts to find that there was a genuine declaration of trust, or to understand why, as there was a resulting trust of the option there was not also a resulting trust of the shares which resulted from the exercise of such option. The practical consequence was that the beneficial interest passed from Vandervell to his children under their settlements which seems very like a disposition.

(e) Where an equitable owner declares a trust of his own interest the position depends on whether or not he has active duties to perform. If A is the trustee and B the beneficiary and B declares a discretionary trust for C and D it will be treated as a valid declaration of trust. If B simply declares a fixed trust for C and D and there are no active duties to perform then he will have assigned his equitable interest in which case the transaction will be invalid unless it satisfies the requirements of section 53(1)(c). Assuming the assignment is valid, B will drop out of the picture and A will hold directly for C and D, *Grainge v. Wilberforce* (1889).

(f) A formal transfer of shares following an oral agreement amounts to an assignment for the purposes of section 53(1)(c) and so used to attract stamp duty. In *Oughtred v. I.R.C.* (H.L., 1960) trustees held shares for the benefit of Mrs Oughtred for life with remainder to her son Peter. In return for some shares of his mother's Peter made an oral contract to transfer his interest in remainder to his mother. Subsequently formal transfers were executed transferring these shares to the mother. The Revenue claimed stamp duty on the transfers as they were the documents which effectively transferred the interest. The argument that the equitable interest passed on the oral contract and that thereafter Peter held on a constructive trust for his mother, so that section 53(1)(c) had no application, was rejected.

(g) Oral agreements, without subsequent written transfers, may be valid as the "creation or operation of resulting, implied or constructive trusts" under section 53(2). In *Neville v. Wilson* (1996) an oral agreement, which constituted each shareholder a constructive trustee for the other shareholders, was upheld.

(h) Where an assignee of an equitable interest is to hold in a fiduciary capacity there is no need for the writing to contain all the terms of the trust (*cf.* where there is a declaration of trust of land which must contain all the terms of the trust). In *Re Tyler* (1967) Miss Tyler, by her will, appointed King and Green executors. Before her death, shortly after making her will, she gave £1,500 to King and later in a letter she wrote to him instructing him to use the money for Green and any surplus as she had previously directed. On the assumption that there was a resulting trust of the money for Miss Tyler after she had paid the money to King, the letter amounted to a valid assignment of that equitable interest.

(i) A disclaimer of an interest does not amount to an assignment. In *Re Paradise Motor Co. Ltd* (1968) a stepfather gave an equitable interest in some shares to his stepson. When the stepson discovered this he made it clear he did not want them. Subsequently he changed his mind. An argument that the disclaimer was ineffective because it was not in writing to comply with section 53 was rejected.

---

4. SECRET TRUSTS

To avoid the statutory provisions for the formal creation of trusts being used as an "engine of fraud" the doctrine of secret trusts was developed. Secret trusts arise mostly in the case of wills.

Once probate is granted, a will becomes a document of public record. It can be inspected by anyone who pays the appropriate fee. Thus a testator who wants to benefit a mistress or an illegitimate child may prefer not to disclose his wishes in his will.

FULLY SECRET TRUSTS

In a fully secret trust it appears from the will that the donee is to take the gift beneficially. An example would be where a testator in his will left Blackacre to Fred absolutely but Fred had previously agreed to the testator's request that he would hold it for Mavis. In such a case Fred will be compelled to carry out the trust. In *Ottaway v. Norman* (1972) the testator agreed with his housekeeper that she could have his bungalow after his death provided she left it to the testator's son and daughter-in-law, Mr and Mrs William Ottaway, after her own death. She agreed to this, so the testator left the bungalow to her absolutely. When later the housekeeper died she left the property to Norman. The court held the plaintiffs were entitled to the property.

The essential element in a secret trust is that the obligation to hold the property on trust must have been accepted by the trustee before the testator's death. This principle is illustrated by *Wallgrave v. Tebbs* (1855). The testator gave money in his will to Tebbs and Martin. After the testator's death a draft letter was found specifying how the testator wanted them to hold the money. The court held that because there had been no communication of this to Tebbs and Martin before the testator's death there was no binding trust. Therefore Tebbs and Martin could take beneficially.

There are difficulties if the gift is to two donees and only one accepts the trust. In *Re Stead* (1901) Farwell J. laid down elaborate rules depending on whether the donees were joint tenants or tenants in common. The better view is that the only question should be "has the gift been made to the donees on the strength of a promise, made by one of them, that the property would be held on the terms of a secret trust?" If so all the donees should be bound.

The donees must know not merely that they are to hold the property on trust but also the terms of the trust, *Re Boyes* (1884). The onus of proving the trust lies on the person seeking to establish it. If donees accept a trust, but only discover its terms after the testator's death, they will hold it for those entitled to the residue, or if the gift is of residue to those entitled on intestacy.

An addition to the trust fund must also be communicated to the trustees. In *Re Colin Cooper* (1939) a testator left £5,000 to trustees on the terms of trust which he had communicated to them. Without telling them he increased the sum to £10,000 by codicil. The first £5,000 was held by them on the terms of the trust but the second was held on a resulting trust.

If an owner of property does not make a will because X, the person entitled on intestacy, has agreed to hold it for a secret beneficiary, then the trust is enforceable against X, *Re Gardner (Huey v. Cunningham)* (1920).

HALF-SECRET TRUSTS

These arise where on the face of the will property is given to X *as trustee* but the *terms* of the trust do not appear in the will. X of course cannot take the property beneficially so there cannot be the same possibility of fraud as in a fully secret trust. Nevertheless, as the trustee has undertaken an obligation binding on his conscience he will be compelled to perform the terms of the trust as accepted by him before the will was made.

The main difference between a fully secret and half-secret trust is that in the latter the communication and acceptance must precede, or be contemporaneous with, the making of the will. This rule is based on some dicta in *Blackwell v. Blackwell* (H.L., 1929). There seems no reason in principle, however, why the communication and acceptance should not be at any time before the testator's death.

The terms of the trust must be sufficiently communicated to the trustee. It is sufficient if he is handed an envelope marked "not to be opened before my death" but he must know that in the envelope are the terms of the secret trust and he must have agreed that he will carry out such terms, whatever they happen to be, *Re Keen* (1937).

In fact in *Re Keen* the half-secret trust failed. The testator left property in his will "upon such trusts as may be notified by me to them (*i.e.* his executors and trustees) during my lifetime." The lady whose name was in the sealed envelope given to the trustees failed in her claim to the property on two grounds. First, the will by referring to future communications fell foul of the principle laid down in *Blackwell v. Blackwell* (H.L., 1929). The testator would, contrary to the Wills Act 1837, by that means reserve to himself a power of making future unwitnessed dispositions of property simply by notifying the trustees. (This argument is misconceived. Secret trusts, as will be explained, operate outside the will and so should not be governed by Wills Act rules.) Secondly, the communication, having in fact been made before the execution of the will, was inconsistent with the terms of the will. The court held therefore that the gift fell into residue.

Distinctions between fully and half-secret trusts

(a) As already mentioned, communication and acceptance in a fully secret trust can be at any time before the testator dies. In a half-secret trust communication and acceptance must be before or at the same time as the execution of the will.

(b) In a fully secret trust it does not matter that the will contradicts the trust. The fact that the trustee appears in the will to take beneficially is itself a contradiction, but to allow the trust to fail on that count would be to undermine the whole basis of secret trusts. In a half-secret trust there can be no conflict between the will and the trust.

(c) Under section 15 of the Wills Act 1837 a beneficiary or beneficiary's spouse who witnesses a will loses his interest. In a fully secret trust the trustee appears to be the beneficiary. It may be therefore that no property will vest in the trustee so that there can be no trust for the secret beneficiaries. On the other hand oral evidence might be permitted to establish the trusteeship, although this is undecided. In a half-secret trust the trustee cannot take beneficially in any event. So it does not matter if he witnesses the will.

(d) If the trustee predeceases the testator in a fully secret trust the trust will probably fail. There is a failure of the legacy on which the trust was to operate, *Re Maddock* (1902). In a half-secret trust where there is clearly a trust set up by the will, equity will not allow the trust to fail for want of a trustee.

Dehors the will

A secret or half-secret trust is said to operate *"dehors"* (outside) the will. In other words the trust arises not from the will but from its communication to, and acceptance by, the trustee. Thus the rules governing wills should not apply, *cf. Re Keen* (1937). As was mentioned in (c) above, under section 15 of the Wills Act 1837 where a beneficiary witnesses a will he loses his interest. He will not do so if he is a beneficiary by virtue of a fully or half-secret trust. In *Re Young* (1951) a testator made a bequest to his wife with a direction that on her death she should leave the property for the purposes he had already communicated to her. One of these purposes was that she should give the chauffeur £2,000. Although the chauffeur had witnessed the will, he was entitled to the money.

A more doubtful illustration of the rule that the trust is created outside the will is *Re Gardner (No. 2)* (1923). A wife left her estate to her husband for life. After his death it was to be held on a secret trust for five named beneficiaries. One of these beneficiaries died before the wife. The personal representatives of the deceased beneficiary were held entitled to the share. This first-instance decision has been heavily criticised. Although the trust was declared before the will, it could not be properly constituted by transferring the property until the testator died. Thus the beneficiary's interest should have lapsed (*i.e.* totally failed) as he was already dead by that time.

Incorporation by reference

It has sometimes been suggested that the rules that communication and acceptance of a half-secret trust must take place before the will is made and that the will must not contradict what actually happened, result from a confusion with the doctrine of incorporation by reference.

For this probate doctrine to apply the will must refer to a specific written document; for example "I devise Blackacre to X on the trusts which I have communicated to him by a letter dated May 2, 1986." This letter is then admitted to probate together with the will. Therefore there is no element of secrecy. The trustee, unlike a trustee in a half-secret trust, does not need to know about the document until the testator dies. The result of the doctrine is that it is as if the document was contained in the will itself. Thus a beneficiary under the document will lose the gift if he witnesses the will (Wills Act 1837, s.15) and the gift will lapse if such a beneficiary predeceases the testator.

Express or constructive trusts

There is much academic controversy over whether a secret trust is an express or constructive trust. It is of no practical consequence except where it is a declaration of trust relating to land which must be evidenced in writing (L.P.A. 1925, s.53(1)(b)—see Chap. 3). In the case of a fully secret trust the courts would never allow the section to operate as a fraud on the secret beneficiary. A half-secret trust may well be classified as an express trust as the will discloses it and it is declared dehors. Moreover, there is no possibility of the trustee taking beneficially. It could therefore be argued that half-secret trusts of land should be in writing. But as it is considered illogical to have distinctions between fully and half-secret trusts the courts might interpret fraud in a wide sense to mean frustrating the testator's intention. Thus they might uphold a half-secret trust of land even in the absence of writing, *cf. Re Baillie* (1886).

5. CONSTITUTION OF TRUSTS

To be enforceable, a trust must be properly constituted. This can be done in two ways; either by an effective transfer to trustees or by a declaration of trust where the property is already vested in the trustee.

Transfer to trustees

The settlor must transfer the property to the trustee in the proper form. To transfer freehold property a conveyance is needed, or a transfer in the case of registered land. Leases are transferred by a deed of assignment. Shares are transferred by an executed transfer form and the name of the new owner being registered on the company's register. Chattels are transferred by physical delivery.

If the correct procedure is not followed the transfer to the trustees will be ineffective. In *Richards v. Delbridge* (1874) Delbridge purported to transfer a lease. He wrote on the back of the lease "this deed and all thereto belonging I give to Edward Burnetto Richards from this time forth with all the stock in trade." The gift failed; there should have been a proper deed of assignment to pass the legal estate, or a declaration of trust. In *Antrobus v. Smith* (1806) an indorsement on the back of a share certificate was ineffective to pass title to the shares. In *Re Fry* (1946) a donor died after executing a share transfer. As he was resident abroad he needed the consent of the Treasury which he had not obtained and so the gift was ineffective. If the donor has done everything he can do to transfer the gift but its effectiveness depends on some act of the donee or a third party, the gift will not fail. In *Re Rose* (1952) the donor executed a share transfer and handed it, together with the share certificate, to the donee. The gift was valid. The donor had no more to do to perfect the gift although the title would not be complete until the shares had been registered by the company in the name of the donee.

There can be an effective assignment of an equitable interest without any need to transfer the legal estate to trustees, *Kekewich v. Manning* (1851). The assignment must be in writing to comply with section 53(1)(c) of the Law of Property Act 1925 (see Chap. 3).

Declaration of trust by the settlor

A settlor with a legal or equitable interest can declare himself a trustee of the property for a beneficiary. He can do this orally except in the case of land when the declaration must be evidenced in writing (L.P.A. 1925, s.53(1)(b)). The settlor can use any form or words or his intention may be inferred from his conduct. In *Paul v. Constance* (1977) Mr Constance received some compensation for an injury at work. Too embarrassed to open a joint account with his mistress, he opened it in his sole name, although he always intended that the money should be shared with her. On his death Mrs Constance, the lawful widow, claimed all the money. It was held that Mr Constance had declared a trust, albeit informally, of the account for himself and his mistress.

However, an ineffective gift will not be construed as a declaration of trust, for the settlor has shown his intention to give the property away. Turner L.J. said in *Milroy v. Lord* (1862) "there is no equity in this court to perfect an imperfect gift."

This is illustrated by the case of *Jones v. Lock* (1865). A father received a whigging from his wife for not bringing a gift for his baby on return from a visit to Birmingham. Thereupon he produced a cheque for £900 made out to himself. He gave it to the child saying "look you here. I give this to baby." The baby then began to tear up the cheque which was removed from him and placed in a safe where it was found after the father's death. It was held to be an imperfect gift for the cheque had not been indorsed. The purported gift was evidence that the father did not intend to declare himself a trustee of the money.

Enforceability of completely and incompletely constituted trusts

1. A completely constituted trust is enforceable by all beneficiaries whether they have given consideration or not.

2. An incompletely constituted trust can be enforced by beneficiaries who have given consideration for equity looks on as done that which has been agreed to be done. The imperfect transfer will be treated as a contract to transfer.

3. If the beneficiaries have not given valuable consideration then they cannot enforce an incompletely constituted trust. Equity will not assist a volunteer. Valuable consideration means money or money's worth or marriage. A settlement made before or in consideration of marriage or one made in fulfilment of an ante-nuptial agreement is made for value. Only certain people are deemed to be within the marriage consideration. They are the husband, wife, children and possibly grandchildren. Contrast *Re Plumptre's Marriage Settlement* (1910) (next-of-kin, being volunteers, could not enforce covenant to settle after-acquired property) with *Pullan v. Koe* (1913)

(children, being within marriage consideration, could enforce a similar covenant).

Problems with future property

1. Definition. Future property is property which is not yet in existence. For example a possibility of obtaining royalties from a book, or inheriting under a will. This must be contrasted with a vested or contingent future interest which has not yet fallen into possession; to A for life, remainder to C if he reaches 25. C's interest, although it may never vest, is already in existence and can be assigned.

2. Assignments of non-existent property. In the absence of consideration, any assignment of property which might be acquired in the future is a nullity. In *Re Ellenborough* (1903) Lord Ellenborough's sister purported to convey by a voluntary settlement the property she would receive under her brother's will. At that time she had only a hope of obtaining the property, for her brother might have changed his will. When her brother died, she refused to transfer to the trustees the property which she received under her brother's will. It was held that the trustees could not compel her to do so. If however, the beneficiary had given consideration, equity would treat the gift as a contract to convey the property when received, if ever.

3. Declarations of trust relating to future property are also void, *Williams v. Commissioners of Inland Revenue* (1965), unless consideration is given when equity will treat such a declaration as a contract to create a trust.

Problems with covenants (*i.e.* agreements made in a deed)

At common law an action in damages will lie for breach of contract where there is consideration or a deed. Equity, however, will only grant specific performance of an agreement where there is consideration.

Suppose S covenants with trustees to settle £20,000 on his mistress M. He then changes his mind, having found a new lady. M cannot enforce the covenant for she is a volunteer. The trustees could sue for breach of covenant but as they have lost nothing they would probably receive only nominal damages. Moreover, trustees will not be compelled to sue for breach of the covenant, *Re Pryce* (1917) and have been directed not to sue, *Re Kay* (1939) because otherwise beneficiaries would be obtaining indirectly what they could not obtain directly.

The cases on covenants are confusing, but the following propositions emerge:

(a) Where there is a covenant, *i.e.* a promise contained in a deed, between the settlor and the beneficiary the beneficiary can sue at common law for damages, *Cannon v. Hartley* (1949).

(b) Where there is a covenant between the settlor and the beneficiary *and* the beneficiary has given valuable consideration, in addition to damages the beneficiary can bring an action for specific performance.

(c) Where there is a covenant with trustees in consideration of marriage, all the beneficiaries within the marriage consideration can enforce the covenant for both existing and after-acquired property.

(d) The settlor can make a covenant with a trustee to the effect that the trustee shall immediately hold the benefit of the covenant for the beneficiary. This is a completely constituted trust of the benefit of the covenant and would be enforceable by a beneficiary who has not given consideration.

In *Fletcher v. Fletcher* (1844) Ellis Fletcher covenanted with trustees to pay them £60,000 to hold for his son Jacob. He never gave the trustees the cash. Jacob succeeded in claiming the money by pleading that there was a completely constituted trust of the promise to pay the £60,000, and that he could enforce the trust of this promise. This case has been much criticised as it does not appear that there was any intention on the part of Ellis or the trustees to create a trust of the promise.

In spite of statements to the contrary in *Re Cook's Settlements Trust* (1965) there is no reason in principle why there should not be a properly constituted trust of the benefit of the covenant (which is a *chose in action*) to settle future property, though in practice it may be difficult to establish the intention that such a covenant should be the subject-matter of the trust.

(c) Where the subject-matter of the trust is the property itself, rather than the benefit of the covenant, the trust is unenforceable by a volunteer beneficiary. This applies to both existing and future property, *Re Cook's Settlement* (1965).

To sum up, a covenant to transfer property is prima facie an unconstituted trust. There has neither been an effective transfer to trustees nor a declaration of trust. Therefore it is unenforceable by the beneficiary unless he has given consideration or is a party to the deed. In some cases it may be possible to establish a completely constituted trust of the benefit of the covenant itself.

Exceptions to the rule that equity will not perfect an imperfect gift

1. A *donatio mortis causa*. This is a gift made in contemplation of death. There is an express or implied condition that the gift will not become absolute until the donor dies. The gift will be perfected at death. It cannot be revoked by will for it is deemed to precede the will.

There are four essentials for a valid *donatio mortis causa*:

(a) There must be at the time of the gift a realistic expectation of imminent death. It does not matter if the donor dies from something different from that which he contemplated, as where he expects to die from cancer but is in fact killed in an air crash.

(b) The gift must be conditional on death. During the life of the donor it can be revoked. On revocation, if the donee has full title to the property, he will hold it on trust for the donor. But if there has been no effective transfer, the property, on revocation, will remain with the donor. If there has been no effective transfer and no revocation the donor's personal representatives will on the death of the donor hold the property on a trust, which arises by operation of law, for the donee.

(c) There must be delivery to the donee of the subject-matter of the gift or something representing it. Oral or written words of a gift are not essential, *Tate v. Hilbert* (1793). Dominion must be given (*i.e.* use and control) not just physical possession. It is possible that words of gift can change the nature of the donee's possession from bailee to a donee under a *donatio mortis causa*, *Woodward v. Woodward* (1995).

(d) The property must be capable of passing by *donatio mortis causa*. Chattels can clearly pass by delivery. Even a key to a safe-box will be a sufficient delivery of its contents. Some *choses in action* can be effected by delivering an appropriate document. Delivery of National Savings Certificates, cheques drawn by third parties, a bank deposit book have all been held to be a sufficient delivery of the property they represent. Some kinds of property cannot pass by *donatio mortis causa*, including the donor's own cheque. This is merely a direction to the bank which, unless the cheque is cashed before the donor dies, will automatically be cancelled on his death. The Court of Appeal has held that land can be the subject-matter of a *donatio mortis causa*, *Sen v. Headley* (1991). There is some doubt about shares in a company; contrast *Re Weston* (1902) with *Staniland v. Willott* (1852).

2. The rule in *Strong v. Bird* (1874). If there is a purported gift to a donee and the donee subsequently obtains property in another capacity then the gift will be deemed perfected. There are two requirements. The donor must have manifested a continuing intention to make a present gift of definite property. The property must become lawfully vested in the donee. For example, where he becomes the donor's personal representative.

3. Proprietary estoppel. Where a donor, who has made an imperfect gift, stands by while the donee improves the property thinking it is or will be his, the courts may in some circumstances compel him to complete the gift, *Pascoe v. Turner* (1979).

4. Conveyance to a minor. A minor cannot hold a legal estate. A purported conveyance is not, however, totally ineffective. It operates as a declaration that the land is held in trust for the minor. Trusts of Land and Appointment of Trustees Act 1996, s.2 Schedule 1.

5. Settlements made by one deed. Section 4 of the Settled Land Act 1925 requires two deeds to constitute a perfect settlement. If there is only one deed then it operates as a trust instrument and the tenant for life is entitled to ask for a vesting deed (S.L.A. 1925, s.9).

---

6. SETTING TRUSTS ASIDE

In some cases a trust may be revoked by the settlor or set aside by a third party.

REVOCATION

The general rule is that once a trust has been completely constituted it cannot be revoked by a settlor. Revocation is possible where:

(a) there is an express power of revocation in the settlement;

(b) the settlor was induced to make the settlement by fraud or undue influence or it was made under some fundamental mistake or misapprehension as to its nature or effect; or

(c) the trust is really only an arrangement for the payment of creditors. This is called an illusory trust (see Chap. 1—*Classification of Trusts*).

TRANSACTIONS DEFRAUDING CREDITORS

There is often a conflict between the claims of a settlor's family and his creditors. As will be seen in Chapter 7 there are permitted ways of protecting property under protective trusts. Although the law strives to let a man do what he wants with his own property, a trust created by a settlor with the intention of defeating his creditors can be set aside.

The law is now contained in the Insolvency Act 1986 but section 172 of the Law of Property Act 1925 and section 42 of the Bankruptcy Act 1914 still apply to trusts created before December 29, 1986.

Section 172 of the Law of Property Act 1925

"Voluntary conveyances to defraud creditors voidable
(1) Save as provided in this section, every conveyance of property made whether before or after the commencement of this Act, with intent to defraud creditors, shall be voidable, at the instance of any person thereby prejudiced.
(2) . . .
(3) This section does not extend to any estate or interest in property conveyed for valuable consideration and in good faith or upon good consideration and in good faith to any person not having, at the time of the conveyance, notice of the intent to defraud creditors."

There are several unsatisfactory points about this section:
(a) although the heading refers to voluntary conveyances, the section itself refers to *every* conveyance;
(b) the reference to good faith in subsection (3) appears to refer to the transferor of the property, who by the very nature of the provision cannot be in good faith. It should be the good faith of the transferee which is at issue;
(c) good consideration means natural love and affection. A debtor hounded by his creditors is most likely to transfer property to his close relations. It is just such transactions which should be set aside. It was assumed in *Re Eicholz* (1959)

that only valuable consideration was sufficient to bring someone within the protection of subsection (3), see also *Lloyds
Bank v. Marcan* (1973).

(d) "conveyance" is defined in section 205(1)(ii). The definitions
presuppose an instrument in writing, although in *Re Eicholz*
(1959) a conveyance was, for the purpose of section 172,
deemed to include an oral transaction.

The effect of an order under section 172 is that the settlement
is only set aside in so far as is necessary to pay the creditors. The
beneficiaries are entitled to the rest, *Ideal Bedding Co. Ltd v. Holland*
(1907).

There are problems in deciding whether a settlor made a settlement "with intent to defraud creditors." This intent does not necessarily involve deceit or dishonesty. The intent will be presumed if
the settlor makes a settlement when he cannot pay his debts without the property settled. The fact that he has debts does not necessarily raise the presumption.

In *Re Wise* (1886) a master mariner jilted his fiancee and married
another. The former started an action for breach of promise of
marriage. At about the time Wise was served with the writ, he
became entitled to a legacy which he at once settled on his wife.
The plaintiff, having obtained judgment against him which he was
unable to pay, made Wise bankrupt. The court refused to set aside
the settlement. At the time Wise made it he was able to pay his
debts without the legacy and he satisfied the court that in making
the settlement he was not influenced by the plaintiff's action.

In *Lloyds Bank Ltd v. Marcan* (1973) the court did find an intention
to deprive a creditor. Marcan was a horticulturist. He mortgaged
his premises to the bank who subsequently started possession proceedings, whereupon Marcan assigned his share in the horticulture
business to his wife and granted her a lease of the premises for 20
years. This was not particularly dishonest. He had obtained counsel's opinion who had said that it was in order. The bank could still
get possession, albeit subject to the lease. The court held that the
lease could be set aside. The value of the premises was diminished
if vacant possession could not be given.

An intention may be presumed where the settlor makes a settlement immediately before entering into a hazardous trade even if
he owes no debts at the time, *Mackay v. Douglas* (1872). In *Re Butter-
worth* (1882) a successful baker made a voluntary settlement before
purchasing a grocer's business, a trade in which he had no experience. He subsequently sold the grocery business for the same price

as he paid for it and continued as a baker. Two years later he became bankrupt. The settlement was set aside.

Subsection (3) gives protection to purchasers for value only if they are in good faith. In *Colombine v. Penhall* (1853) a man had been living with a woman for several years. In order to put his property outside the reach of his creditors he settled the property on his mistress in consideration of marriage and married her. The settlement was set aside. The whole purpose of the marriage was to defeat the creditors. Had the settlement given any interest to the children of the marriage that interest would not have been available to the creditors. The children would have been innocent purchasers.

Sections 423–425 of the Insolvency Act 1986

Section 172 has been repealed by the Insolvency Act 1986 and replaced by sections 423–425 of that Act. The sections give the court power to make various orders where it is satisfied that a transaction was entered into at an undervalue for the purpose of putting assets beyond the reach of the person making (or who may at some time make) the claim or otherwise prejudicing his interests. Undervalue includes:

(a) making a gift;
(b) entering into a transaction without consideration;
(c) entering into a transaction in consideration of marriage; and
(d) accepting a consideration which does not reflect the true value of the property.

The only persons protected against the effect of orders under these sections are third parties (those who are not parties to the transaction and do not receive property from the debtor direct) who acquire property, or a benefit from the transaction, in good faith and for value without notice of the circumstances which gave rise to the order.

The old case law on section 172 will presumably be applied in deciding whether a transaction was entered into for the purpose of debt avoidance.

In *Agricultural Mortgage Corp v. Woodward* (1995) a farmer, whose land was charged to the AMC, granted a tenancy to his wife so that the mortgagee would not be able to sell the land with vacant possession. Although the wife paid a full market rent this was treated as a transaction at an undervalue and set aside. The benefit the wife acquired was far greater than the rent she paid, for she was in a position to demand a ransom for surrendering her tenancy.

BANKRUPTCY

Section 42 of the Bankruptcy Act 1914

Even where there is no fraud, voluntary settlements can sometimes be set aside on the subsequent bankruptcy of the settlor.

1. Two years. If the settlor went bankrupt within two years after the date of the settlement it could be set aside by the trustee in bankruptcy even where the settlor was solvent at the time of the settlement.

2. Ten years. If the settlor goes bankrupt within 10 years after the date of the settlement it can be set aside unless those claiming under the settlement can prove that the settlor could pay his debts at the time of the settlement without the property comprised in the settlement and that the property passed to the trustees at that time.

Section 42 does not apply to settlements made before and in consideration of marriage, nor to those made in favour of a purchaser in good faith for valuable consideration.

Sections 339–342 of the Insolvency Act 1986

These sections replaced section 42 of the Bankruptcy Act 1914. They give the court wide powers to make such orders as it thinks fit, including setting aside settlements, on the application of the trustee in bankruptcy where an individual is adjudged bankrupt and has previously entered into transactions at an undervalue or given a preference to someone.

1. Transactions at an undervalue. These are defined in the same way as for section 423.

Two years. If a bankruptcy petition is presented within two years of any such transaction then an order can be made in respect of it notwithstanding that the individual was solvent at the time.

Five years. If a bankruptcy petition is presented within five years of any such transaction then an order can be made in respect of it unless the individual can prove that he was solvent at the time without the property included in the transaction. There will be a rebuttable presumption of insolvency where the transaction was entered into with an associate. An associate is exhaustively defined in section 435 of the Act and includes spouses, relatives, partners and employers.

2. Preference. A preference occurs where by some act an individual puts one of his creditors, or a surety or guarantor of his debts, in a better position, should the individual's bankruptcy ensue, then he would have otherwise been in. The court can only make an order where the individual was "influenced in deciding to give" the preference "by a desire to produce" this result. This will be presumed, unless the contrary is shown, where preference is given to an associate.

Six months. The court can make an order relating to a preference given in the six months preceding the bankruptcy petition unless the individual was solvent at the time without the property included in the preference.

Two years. Where the preference is given to an associate the court can make an order relating to a preference given in the two years preceding the bankruptcy petition unless the individual was solvent at the time without the property included in the preference.

An individual who enters into a transaction at an undervalue or gives a preference is insolvent for the purposes of section 341 if:

"(a) he is unable to pay his debts as they fall due; or (b) the value of his assets is less than the amount of his liabilities, taking into account his contingent and prospective liabilities."

Protection is given to third parties who acquire property from someone, other than the individual who has entered into the transaction at an undervalue or given the preference, provided that they are in good faith, and have given value. Anybody fulfilling those conditions who acquires a benefit from a transaction will not have to pay any sums to the trustee in bankruptcy unless he was a party to the transaction or a creditor at the time of the preference.

SECTION 37 OF THE MATRIMONIAL CAUSES ACT 1973

Where the court is satisfied that one spouse is about to make a disposition with the intention of depriving the other of financial relief under the Act it can make an order protecting the applicant's claim. Dispositions already made can be set aside unless made for valuable consideration to a bona fide purchaser without notice of any intention to defeat the applicant's claim.

SECTION 10 OF THE INHERITANCE (PROVISION FOR FAMILY AND DEPENDANTS) ACT 1975

The court has a discretionary power to make provisions for spouses and other dependants who have not been adequately provided for under the deceased's will or according to the rules of intestacy. In order to defeat such an attempt to claim his estate the deceased might during his lifetime have given away his property. Section 10 provides that donees of gifts made with that intent within six years before the deceased died can be ordered to provide sums of money, or other property not exceeding the value of the gift, in order that financial provision can be made.

7. PROTECTIVE TRUSTS

A protective trust is employed when the settlor wishes to protect property against an improvident beneficiary and the claims of his creditors. The main beneficiary is given a determinable life interest which upon forfeiture is followed by a discretionary trust for a class of beneficiaries of whom he may be one.

DETERMINABLE LIFE INTEREST

Nature of a determinable life interest

One of the difficult problems of property law is understanding the distinction between conditional interests and determinable interests. A determinable interest is a limited interest; its limit being set from the outset. A conditional interest is a full interest which is liable to be cut short by a condition subsequent, with the result that the interest may never run its full course. In practice the easiest way of distinguishing the two is in the words used. Words such as "while," "during," "as long as" and "until" indicate a determinable interest. Words such as "on condition that," "provided that" indicate a conditional interest. The importance of the distinction is that the court does not favour conditional interests which are viewed as forfeitures. A gift to a beneficiary provided that, or on condition that, he does not become bankrupt is void. A gift to a beneficiary until he becomes bankrupt is perfectly valid unless it is the settlor's own bankruptcy he is attempting to guard against.

In *Re Burroughs and Fowler* (1916) the settlor by an ante-nuptial settlement settled property on trust to pay the income to himself for life or until certain events should happen, one of which was bankruptcy. He went bankrupt whereupon his trustee in bankruptcy became entitled to his life interest.

The settlor can protect himself against events other than bankruptcy. In *Re Detmold* (1889) there was a marriage settlement of the settlor's own property until his bankruptcy or until he should suffer "something whereby the same would, by operation of law become payable to some other person" and after such determination on trust to pay the income to his wife. A judgment creditor was appointed. Then the settlor was declared bankrupt. The wife was held entitled to the income because by the time he was bankrupt his determinable interest had already ended.

Events which give rise to forfeiture

It is in the interests of the beneficiary with the determinable life interest to allege that a forfeiture has taken place. His interest will not then vest in the trustee in bankruptcy but will be available for the beneficiaries under the discretionary trust.

The cases given below illustrate in what circumstances forfeiture has been held to have occurred.

In *Re Balfour's Settlement* (1938) the trustees had advanced money to a life tenant in breach of trust. The trustees asserted the right to retain future income to make good the breach of trust. The life tenant went bankrupt. It was held that the trustee in bankruptcy had no claim to the life interest as it had already determined.

In *Re Gourins Will Trusts* (1943) the life tenant ceased to be entitled to receive the income of a trust because she lived in enemy territory during the Second World War. This amounted to a forfeiture and the discretionary trust came into operation, so that the Custodian of Enemy Property could not claim her interest. On the other hand in *Re Hall* (1944) the Custodian was entitled. The trust provided expressly that forfeiture was only to operate if the *annuitant* should "do or suffer any act" whereby the annuity should be payable elsewhere. Her failure to receive the annuity did not arise from her own act but merely from the rules governing residents in enemy territory, so there was no forfeiture.

Under the Matrimonial Causes Act 1973 the Family Division of the High Court can make an order altering a protected life interest under a settlement. In *Re Richardson's Will Trusts* (1958) the court ordered that the principal beneficiary should charge his interest with an annual payment of £50 in favour of his divorced wife. It was held that this amounted to a forfeiture. However, in *General Accident Fire and Life Assurance Corp. Ltd v. I.R.C.* (1963) an order of the court diverting part of the income

from a life tenant in favour of a former wife did not amount to
a forfeiture. This decision is preferable. Forfeiture is concerned
with protecting a spendthrift life tenant against his creditors not
against his former wife.

DISCRETIONARY TRUSTS

Although in this context the purpose of discretionary trusts is to
divert money after a determinable life interest has ended, discretionary trusts are useful outside protective trusts. Before the Finance Act 1975 discretionary trusts were used as estate duty saving
schemes. Today they are still important for exercising control over
the young and improvident and to provide flexibility. The circumstances of the beneficiaries may change, including their liability to
tax.

The essence of a discretionary trust is that the beneficiary has
no right to any part of the income. The trustees have a discretionary power to pay him or apply property for his benefit as
they think fit. Thus except as so far as money has actually been
paid to him, there is no property which his creditors can claim,
Re Coleman (1888).

STATUTORY PROTECTIVE TRUSTS

As has been explained a protective trust can be created expressly
by creating a determinable life interest followed by a discretionary
trust. Since 1925 the settlor can, merely by stating that the income
shall be held on protective trusts, imply all the terms contained in
section 33 of the Trustee Act 1925.

The section provides:

> "Where any income, including an annuity or other periodical income
> payment, is directed to be held on protective trusts for the benefit of
> any person ... for the period of his life or for any less period, then
> during that period ... the said income shall, without prejudice to any
> prior interest, be held on the following trusts, ...
>
> (i) Upon trust for the principal beneficiary during the trust period
> or until he ... does or attempts to do or suffers any act or thing,
> or until any event happens, other than an advance under any
> statutory or express power, whereby, if the said income were pay-
> able during the trust period to the principal beneficiary absolutely
> during that period, he would be deprived of the right to receive
> the same or any part thereof, in any of which cases, as well as on
> the termination of the trust period, whichever first happens, this
> trust of the said income shall fail or determine;
>
> (ii) If the trust aforesaid fails or determines ... the said income shall

be held upon trust for the application thereof for the maintenance or support, or otherwise for the benefit, of all or any one or
more exclusively . . . of the following persons . . .
  (a) the principal beneficiary and his . . . wife, if any, and his . . .
      children . . . or;
  (b) if there is no (spouse) or issue . . . the principal beneficiary
      and the persons who would, if he were actually dead, be
      entitled to the trust property . . .
as the trustees in their absolute discretion . . . think fit."

8. RESULTING TRUSTS

These trusts are called resulting because the beneficial interest in
the property results back to the settlor, or if he is dead, to his
estate. Sometimes they are called implied trusts for they are not
express but arise from the deemed intention of the settlor. The
trusts set out immediately below are sometimes referred to as automatic resulting trusts while those on p. 37 (purchase in the name
of another) and p. 40 (voluntary transfer or conveyance from
existing owner of property to another) as presumed resulting
trusts. See Megarry J. in *Re Vandervell (No. 2)* (1974).

THE BENEFICIAL INTERESTS ARE NOT EXHAUSTED BY THE EXPRESS TRUSTS

Failure of beneficiary

If a settlor conveys property on trust for A for life and then to
A's children absolutely and A never has any children then the
remainder will result back to the settlor. This must be contrasted
with the position where trustees hold for A absolutely and he then
dies without making a will and no relation is entitled to succeed
him under intestacy rules. In that case there is no question of the
property resulting to the settlor for he has parted with his whole
interest. The property will go to the Crown as *bona vacantia*.

Trusts partially expressed

If the settlor has conveyed property on trust for A for life and
made no other provision then on A's death the property would
result back to the settlor (or his estate if he were dead). In *Vandervell v. I.R.C.* (H.L., 1967) the Vandervell trustees were given a trust

of an option to purchase some shares. As the terms of the trust
were not spelt out there was an immediate resulting trust for the
settlor, Mr. Vandervell.

Trusts are void

The trusts may turn out to be void as being against public policy
or offending the perpetuity rule. There will then be a resulting
trust. In *Re Diplock* (H.L., 1951) there was a gift of residue in a will
"for purposes which the trustees consider to be charitable." This
was a void direction for charitable purposes. So the gift resulted to
those who would have been entitled if the testator had died intestate as far as that property was concerned.

Surplus funds

Sometimes surplus funds will result to the settlor. In *Re The
Trusts of the Abbott Fund* (1900) money was collected for two deaf
and dumb old ladies. They had no rights in the capital. When they
died the money was held on a resulting trust for the subscribers.
However, often the beneficiaries will be deemed entitled to all the
funds. It depends on the construction of the gift. In *Re Andrews Trust*
(1905) money was subscribed "for or towards" the education of the
infant children of a deceased clergyman. On the completion of their
education they were held entitled to all the money in equal shares.
A similar result was achieved in *Re Osoba* (1979). A gift was made
to the testator's widow "for her maintenance and for the training
of my daughter up to university grade and for the maintenance of
my aged mother." The mother predeceased the testator. The
widow died and the daughter completed her education. It was held
that the widow and the daughter took as joint tenants so that the
daughter succeeded to the whole fund on the death of the widow.
The references to education and maintenance were only explana-
tions of the motive for the gift.

Problems arise when money is collected in collecting boxes from
the passing public. In *Re Gillingham Bus Disaster Fund* (1958) a fund
was set up following a disaster when marine cadets were mown
down by a bus. The collection was for the disabled and thereafter
for worthy causes. (Worthy causes is not sufficient to constitute a
charitable purpose.) Too much money was collected. The judge
held that the surplus funds should result to the subscribers and
where they could not be found the money was paid into court.

Surplus funds often arise on the dissolution of an unincorporated
society (see Chap. 10). In *Re Printers and Transferers Society* (1899) a
society was founded to raise funds for strikes and benefits for its

members by weekly subscriptions. There was no provision for what was to happen on dissolution. The court held there was a resulting trust for the *existing* members at the time of the dissolution.

In *Re Hobourne Aero Components Ltd's Air Raid Disaster Fund* (1946) the surplus funds were held on a resulting trust for anyone who had ever contributed according to his contribution, making allowance for any benefits received.

Another method of dealing with surplus funds is to interpret the contribution to the society as an out-and-out transfer. Thus on the dissolution of the society there would be no one the surplus could go to, and it would therefore go to the Crown as *bona vacantia*, *Cunnack v. Edwards* (1895).

In *Re West Sussex Constabulary's Widows, Children and Benevolent (1930), Fund Trusts (1971)* money was received for the fund from donations, collecting boxes and proceeds of entertainment. It was held that: (a) the money from identifiable donations should go on a resulting trust; (b) that the money from collecting boxes was an outright gift and should go to the Crown as *bona vacantia*; and (c) that the proceeds of the entertainments should also go *bona vacantia*. Those who had purchased tickets had received what they paid for and there was no question of them claiming the money back.

However in the later case of *Re Bucks. Constabulary Widow's and Orphan's Fund Friendly Society* (1979) Walton J. held that voluntary subscriptions were an accretion to the funds of the society and should be distributed amongst those members who still belonged to the society at the date of dissolution.

The modern approach has been to follow this case and treat the rights of the members as contractual according to the society's constitution rather than imposing a trust. This trend was not followed though by Scott J. in *Davis v. Richards & Wallington Industries Ltd* (1991). Whilst accepting that a resulting trust could be excluded expressly or by implication he did not consider that a payment under a contract was sufficient to exclude the resulting trust. Surplus funds which were derived from employers' contributions to a pension fund should be held on a resulting trust. The resulting trust was excluded as far as the employee's contributions were concerned because (a) it was impracticable to make the payments and (b) the financial return from the fund exceeded the legislative maximum. A resulting trust was also excluded where funds had been obtained from other companies because it had been made plain that the trustees of the pension funds of those companies were divesting themselves completely of the transferred funds. On the facts of the case there was no surplus because it was held that the deed purporting to deal with the surplus was valid.

PURCHASE IN THE NAME OF ANOTHER

Presumption of resulting trust to real purchaser

Where V sells property to P but the purchase money is provided by B, P will hold the property for B. Parol evidence is admissible to prove that the money was really paid by B even in the case of land. Section 53(1) of the Law of Property Act 1925, which requires declarations of trusts of land to be in writing, does not apply to resulting trusts.

There will also be a resulting trust where two people provide the purchase price but the property is taken in the name of one of them only. For instance where the matrimonial home is conveyed into the name of the husband alone but the wife made a contribution to the purchase price, he will hold the legal estate on trust for himself and his wife. The contribution must relate to the acquisition of the property. It may be direct as where she pays the deposit, or part of the balance of the purchase price, or some of the mortgage instalments. It may be indirect as where she pays other household expenses to enable her husband to pay the mortgage instalments. But the intention that she should have an interest must exist at the time of acquisition. This intention need not be express; it can be inferred from conduct, even subsequent conduct, but an intention cannot be imputed to the parties, *Gissing v. Gissing* (H.L., 1971). A wife or mistress will not acquire an interest in the home merely by doing the housework and bringing up the children, *Burns v. Burns* (1984).

Improvements contemplated at the time of the acquisition and subsequently carried out by the non-legal owner can give him an interest. But if there is no such intention, improvements will not result in an interest unless there is proprietary estoppel. This occurs for example where B is encouraged to work on A's land in the expectation of receiving some interest therein. The interest given to him will not necessarily be an interest under a trust. It could be a charge on the property, a licence or even the fee simple absolute, *Pascoe v. Turner* (1979). A *substantial* improvement made by a spouse can result in a share under a trust, section 37 of the Matrimonial Proceedings and Property Act 1970, but the Act applies only to spouses.

On a divorce, the courts have had since 1971 a wide discretion to allocate all the spouses' property regardless of strict property principles. In the case of other joint owners the size and value of the shares must be ascertained. The beneficial interest is proportionate to the contribution but this may be difficult to ascertain in the case of indirect contributions. The valuation of the share is prima facie taken at the date of the sale, although it depends on all the circumstances of the case, *Gordon v. Douce* (1983).

Presumption of advancement

Sometimes the settlor will have made it clear that he intends to make a gift of the property to the persons to whom it is conveyed. In relationships where the donor is under an obligation to provide for the donee, such an intention will be presumed.

1. Wife. A husband who buys property and has it conveyed into the name of his wife or contributes to the mortgage payments of property owned by her is presumed to have intended a gift, *Silver v. Silver* (1958). However, this presumption is easily rebutted today when a wife has earnings of her own. Often, of course, a conveyance is taken in the joint names of the husband and wife with both of them having made a contribution to the purchase money.

If the wife contributes all the money and the property is conveyed into the name of the husband, there is no presumption of a gift. He will, in the absence of evidence to the contrary, be deemed to be holding on trust for her.

2. Child. If a father buys property and has it put into the name of his child then it is presumed he intended a gift, *Dyer v. Dyer* (1788). The presumption does not apply to nephews or sons-in-law. The older cases indicate that there is no presumption of gift where a mother pays the purchase money and the property is in the name of the child. This was because at common law there was no obligation on a mother to support her child. Today it is likely that the courts would find evidence to support a gift, where that was the intention, rather than a resulting trust.

3. In loco parentis. The same presumption of advancement applies where someone has taken on the obligation of providing for a child, for example a stepson or grandchild, *Re Paradise Motor Co. Ltd* (1968).

Rebutting the presumptions

Both the presumption of a resulting trust and the presumption of advancement are only presumptions and so can be rebutted.

Evidence from all the surrounding circumstances will be taken into account. In the case of land, an express declaration of trust will be conclusive in the absence of fraud and there will be no room for the presumption of a resulting trust, *Goodman v. Gallant* (1986). It was held, however, in *Huntingdon v. Hobbs* (1992) that the words in a transfer "the transferees declare that the survivor of them can give a valid receipt for capital money arising on a disposition of land" did not amount to an express declaration of trust that the transferees were beneficial joint tenants. Therefore the beneficial interests were determined on the basis of resulting and constructive trusts. An express declaration, however, will not prejudice those who contributed to the purchase of property but were not parties to the deed, *City of London Building Society v. Flegg* (1988).

It used to be considered that acts and declarations made by the parties before or at the time of the purchase could be taken into account, but that subsequent acts and declarations were admissible as evidence only against the party who made them and not in his favour, *Shephard v. Cartwright* (H.L., 1955). It seems that the Civil Evidence Act 1968 has altered this. Subsequent statements by both parties would be admitted.

Warrent v. Gurney (1944) was a case where the presumption of advancement was rebutted. A father bought a house which was conveyed into the name of his daughter. The father retained the deeds. On his death the daughter claimed to be the beneficial owner of the house. She failed. The retention of the deeds plus other evidence at the time of the purchase rebutted the intention to make a gift.

Elderly parents might put their property into the names of their children for convenience where they do not want to be bothered with the legal formalities, *City of London Building Society v. Flegg* (1985) or where the father would not be accepted as mortgagor *McGrath v. Wallis* (1995). This would not be intended to be a gift.

The presumption of advancement however, is not rebuttable if the reason for the transaction was an improper purpose. If a husband puts property into the name of a wife or child to avoid tax he cannot then rebut the presumption of advancement to claim an interest under a resulting trust. See *Re Emery's Investment Trust* (1959). However, where the improper purpose is not carried into effect the presumption of advancement may be rebutted by showing the reason for the transaction, *Tribe v. Tribe* (1995).

Where a resulting trust is presumed a party cannot defeat that presumption by showing an improper purpose. In *Tinsley v. Milligan* (1993) two lovers bought a house which was registered in the name of T as sole legal owner in order that M might make fraudulent claims for social security benefits. When T and M subsequently quarrelled, M sought a declaration that the house was held by T on trust for the parties in equal shares. It was held by the House of Lords that had the presumption of advancement applied M could not have rebutted that presumption, since to do so would have required reliance on the illegal purpose of the trust. Since the presumption was not applicable, and in the absence of evidence to the contrary, a resulting trust was implied, the underlying illegal nature of the transaction being irrelevant to the claim.

VOLUNTARY TRANSFER OR CONVEYANCE FROM EXISTING OWNER OF PROPERTY TO ANOTHER

The presumption of advancement, and its rebuttal, applies in the same way as it does in the previous situations considered where there is a purchase in the name of another. Whether or not there is a resulting trust is not so clear.

Land

Section 60(3) of the Law of Property Act 1925 provides:

> "In a voluntary conveyance a resulting trust for the grantor shall not be implied merely by reason that the property is not expressed to be conveyed for the use of benefit of the grantee."

It is still possible to find a resulting trust where no gift was intended. In *Hodgson v. Marks* (C.A., 1971) Mrs Hodgson, an old lady, was persuaded to transfer her house to her lodger, Mr Evans, on the understanding that she would continue to be the beneficial owner. When he subsequently sold it to a purchaser, her interest was held to be binding on the purchaser. She was in occupation and had a beneficial interest under a resulting trust which amounted to an overriding interest.

Personalty

On the voluntary transfer of pure personalty there will be a resulting trust unless either there is an express intention to make a gift or the presumption of advancement applies.

In *Re Vinogradoff* (1935) a grandmother transferred War Loan stock into the names of herself and her four-year-old granddaughter to whom she did not stand *in loco parentis*. The court held that there was a resulting trust for the grandmother. This case has been heavily criticised. If no gift was intended, the whole exercise seems pointless.

---

9. CONSTRUCTIVE TRUSTS

It is not possible to give a definition of constructive trusts which would cover all the situations where a constructive trust has been held to exist. A definition given by Snell and cited with approval by Edmund Davies L.J. in *Carl Zeiss Stiftung v. Herbert Smith & Co. (No. 2)* (1967) is "a constructive trust is a trust which is imposed by equity in order to satisfy the demands of justice and good conscience without reference to any express or presumed intention of the parties."

THE TRADITIONAL CONCEPT OF THE CONSTRUCTIVE TRUST

Where there is an existing fiduciary relationship equity will impose, in certain circumstances, a trust on persons who receive trust property even though they are not the trustees of the original trust, or a trust on additional property where existing trustees make a profit from their trust. The most important instances of this type of constructive trust are given below.

Strangers to the trust

1. Knowing receipt or dealing. A distinction must be made between personal liability and a liability *in rem*.

(a) Liability in rem: a beneficiary of the original trust has a proprietary remedy where property is received by a person in breach of trust and may recover the property from that person unless he is a bona fide purchaser of a legal interest for value without notice of the breach of trust. Thus an innocent volunteer will be bound to restore any property, or its proceeds, which is still in his possession even though he had no knowledge of the breach of trust.

(b) Liability *in personam*: a beneficiary may wish to establish a personal liability where, for example, a stranger dealt with trust property but never actually had it in his own hands. In such a case the proprietary remedy would be of no assistance.

It used to be considered that a person would be liable as a constructive trustee where he "has received trust property with actual or *constructive* notice that it is trust property transferred in breach of trust, or because (not being a bona fide purchaser for value without notice) he acquires notice subsequent to such receipt and then deals with the property in a manner inconsistent with the trust," *Karak Rubber Co. Ltd v. Burden (No. 2)* (1972), *per* Brightman J.

However, more modern cases have stressed that liability should be based on "want of probity", *e.g. Re Montague's Settlement Trusts* (1987) *Eagle Trust plc v. SBC Securities Ltd* (1991).

An agent will not be liable as a constructive trustee merely because he is in possession of property which he knows to be trust property, *Williams-Ashman v. Price and Williams* (1942). He would of course be liable if he knew (or, possibly, ought to have known) that it was transferred to him in breach of trust.

Where a solicitor incurs liability as a constructive trustee his partners will not be liable merely because money passes through the firm's client account, *Re Bell's Indenture* (1980). Any money, however, which remains in the account, can be recovered. A partner of the firm would be liable if he had notice of the breach of trust.

2. Accessory Liability. In this case the property is not vested in the stranger. It is not, therefore, correct to say that he is liable as a constructive trustee. He has rather a personal liability to account.

In *Barnes v. Addy* (1874) Lord Selbourne said that in order to be liable a stranger must have assisted "with knowledge in a dishonest and fraudulent design on the part of the trustees".

This statement has been rejected by the Privy Council in *Royal Brunei Airlines v. Tan* (1995). It was held that where a third party dishonestly assisted a trustee to commit a breach of trust, or procured him to do so that third party would be liable irrespective of whether the trustee had been dishonest or fraudulent. Honesty was to be judged objectively, taking into account all the circumstances known to the third party at the time and his particular experience and intelligence.

In *Brinks v. Abu-Saleh* (1995) a wife knew that her husband was carrying money as part of a dishonest transaction but she did not know the true origin of the money. She was held not liable.

Profit from the trust

A trustee must not profit from his trust. Any profit he does make will be held on a constructive trust for the beneficiaries. This is discussed in Chapter 13 on trustees' duties.

Specifically enforceable contract for sale

Once a contract for the sale of land has been made, the beneficial ownership of the property passes to the purchaser and the vendor is deemed to hold the legal estate on a constructive trust for him. It is, however, a qualified trusteeship, The trustee is entitled to possession and to rents and profits until completion and is liable for expenses. Normally trustees are not entitled to profits but are entitled to reclaim expenses. Moreover if the contract is never completed, it is as though the vendor never was a trustee so he cannot be made liable for breach of his trustee-type duties.

Mutual wills

Mutual wills arise where two persons make an arrangement to make similar wills disposing of their property in a particular way. The mere fact that they leave similar wills is not enough. In *Re Oldham* (1925) a husband and wife left property to each other with the same provision should the other predecease. There was no evidence that there was any arrangement or agreement that the wills should be irrevocable. After the husband died the wife remarried and made another will. The second will was upheld. If, however, there had been such an arrangement either party could withdraw from it before the first death; but once the first person has died, the survivor holds the property on an implied or constructive trust for the beneficiaries named in the will. If the survivor makes a second will, his personal representatives will hold the property on the trusts of the first will.

So (assuming an arrangement) if in A's will property is left to B for life with remainder to C and in B's will property is left to A for life with remainder to C, on A's death B is bound by the arrangement. Even if C dies before B his estate will benefit because after the death of A the trust set up by B's will is irrevocable, *Re Haggar* (1930). Although a survivor may alter his will, because a will is inherently revocable, his personal representative will take the property subject to the trust. It is not necessary that the second testator to die should have obtained a personal financial benefit under the will of the first testator to die, *Re Dale's Estate* (1993).

There are difficulties in establishing what property is bound by the trust. The wills themselves may make the position clear. If not it may be that the trust covers only the property which the survivor receives from the estate of the first to die; or to that property and also the property the survivor owned at that time; or even to all the property the survivor owned when he died. In *Re Cleaver* (1981) it was held that a survivor could in his lifetime enjoy the property as an absolute owner "subject to a fiduciary duty which, so to speak, crystallised on his death and disabled him only from voluntary dispositions *inter vivos.*"

Where there are mutual wills a floating trust is created which will not be overturned by the second testator's remarriage. *Goodman v. Goodman* (1996)

Secret trusts

As discussed in Chapter 4 some writers treat secret trusts as constructive trusts.

Conveyance by fraud

Where there is a conveyance *inter vivos* induced by fraud the transferee may be held to hold the property as a constructive trustee for the transferor or some third party, *Rochefoucauld v. Boustead* (1897).

NEW MODEL CONSTRUCTIVE TRUST

In many American jurisdictions the constructive trust is seen as a remedy. It is a means of demanding the return of property to prevent unjust enrichment. In England the constructive trust has always been regarded as a substantive trust imposing on the trustee a duty to hold the trust property on trust for the beneficiaries. The new model constructive trust is similar to the American but has been imposed in a much more discretionary manner.

In the words of Lord Denning in *Hussey v. Palmer* (1972) "It is a trust imposed by law wherever justice and good conscience require it. It is a liberal process, founded on large principles of equity. . . . It is an equitable remedy by which the court can enable an aggrieved party to obtain restitution."

Arguments against the use of the remedial constructive trust include the following:

(a) It is a "last ditch" attempt to find a reason for giving judgment in favour of the plaintiff when there are no established legal principles for doing so.

(b) It is a form of "palm-tree" justice. Nothing is certain and no reliance can be placed on precedent.

(c) The interests of third parties are prejudiced. Creditors cannot claim the trust property if the trustee becomes insolvent. Purchasers will be bound by constructive notice of the beneficiaries' interests (or in the case of registered title by overriding interests where the beneficiaries are in actual occupation) in circumstances where it is impractical or impossible to discover such interests.

There are no clear guidelines when a constructive trust will be implied. Many of the cases are concerned with finding a just solution to informal family arrangements which turn sour.

One way of looking at the cases is to consider them historically. The orthodox trust principles were expressed by the House of Lords in *Gissing v. Gissing* (1970). The essentials for establishing a constructive trust were stated to be (1) that at the time the property is acquired the parties must have intended that the non-legal owner should have a beneficial interest and (2) that the non-legal owner should have made a contribution to the property or acted in some way to his detriment in the belief that he had such an interest. Although the court can infer an intention from conduct, even subsequent conduct, the House of Lords stressed that the court cannot impute to the parties intentions concerning the beneficial ownership which they never had.

Then came the Denning era with the desire to achieve a just solution, regardless of strict legal principles. The post-1984 cases, on the whole, show a return to more traditional trust law.

Two extreme Denning cases are *Heseltine v. Heseltine* (1971) and *Hussey v. Palmer* (1972). In the first case a wife transferred £40,000 to her husband to enable him to qualify as a Lloyds Underwriter and also to equalise their property for estate duty purposes. Any presumption of a *resulting* trust should thereby have been rebutted. Nevertheless the Court of Appeal upheld the claim of the wife to the property on the ground that it would be inequitable for the husband to keep the money. It seems that a constructive trust was found to reach a just solution.

Hussey v. Palmer (1972) concerned a mother who went to live with her daughter and son-in-law. She built an extension at her own expense. Subsequently there was a quarrel. Mrs Hussey moved out. Lord Denning (although the money for the extension had been agreed to be a loan only) held there was a constructive trust in favour of the mother so that she had an interest in the property proportionate to her contribution.

On the other hand, the approach of Lord Denning in *Eves v. Eves* (1975) has been followed by the Court of Appeal in *Grant v. Edwards* (1986). In *Eves v. Eves* a cohabiting couple bought a house. It was conveyed into the sole name of Eves because the woman with whom he lived was under 21. He explained that this was the only reason the house was not taken in joint names. She bore him two children, and did a lot of work in the house and garden before he deserted her. The court held she was entitled to a quarter share. In the more recent case of *Grant v. Edwards* the Court of Appeal again found for the woman where a false reason was given for the house not being put in joint names. In the expectation of acquiring a beneficial interest the woman made substantial contributions to the family expenses which enabled the man to keep up the mortgage instalments. She was therefore entitled under a constructive trust.

Perhaps the contrast in the two cases is what is required to show detriment. Lord Denning required very little detriment to be shown (see *Greasley v. Cooke* (1980)). Recent cases demand a higher degree of detriment. In *Midland Bank Ltd v. Dobson* (1986) a woman failed on this ground to establish a constructive trust. Detriment, however, was found in *Re Basham* (1986) where a stepfather had given the plaintiff assurances that she would benefit from his estate. Thus, a constructive trust was found even though her belief concerned future non-specific assets.

It must be emphasised that an intention to share must be shown. In *Burns v. Burns* a woman who had brought up two children and done the housework for over 17 years was unable to claim an interest in the property because of the absence of such an intention.

In *Lloyds Bank v. Rosset* (1990) the House of Lords reaffirmed the need for an express agreement or arrangement at the time of the purchase, or exceptionally at some later date, that the beneficial interest in the property should be jointly owned. The House of Lords found no such agreement, nor did they find any contribution by the wife to the purchase price or mortgage instalments to give her an interest under a resulting trust.

One of Lord Denning's contributions to the law was the licence coupled with a constructive trust. He held in *Binions v. Evans* (1972) that a purchaser was bound by a licence given to a widow to live in the property. He had bought the property subject to her interest and had paid a lower price as a consequence. This case was followed by Browne-Wilkinson J. in *Re Sharpe* (1980). An elderly aunt made a loan to her nephew to enable him to buy a home and newsagent business. It was agreed that until the loan was repaid she should live in the property. On her nephew's bankruptcy it was held that the effect of the arrangement was to confer on her a licence giving rise to a constructive trust binding on a trustee in bankruptcy.

A constructive trust was imposed in *Peffer v. Rigg* (1972). A purchaser was bound by an interest under a trust for sale of which he had notice but which was not protected under the Land Registration Act 1925. This case was much criticised as notice should have no part to play in registered land. Nevertheless, in *Lyus v. Prowsa Developments* (1982) a constructive trust was again imposed on a purchaser of registered land, where he had bought expressly subject to the plaintiff's unregistered contractual rights.

The modern approach is to be found in *Anstalt v. Arnold* (1988). The case reaffirms that contractual licences are only personal rights. A constructive trust should be imposed only where it is appropriate to do so, on the particular facts. Thus *Re Sharpe* and *Peffer v. Rigg* should not give rise to a constructive trust; *Binions v. Evans* and *Lyus v. Prowsa Developments* should. In the *Binions v. Evans* case the purchaser's conscience was bound; he bought expressly subject to the widow's interest and paid a lower price for the property. Likewise in the *Lyus v. Prowsa Developments* case the property was bought expressly subject to the fresh rights conferred on the plaintiffs.

---

10. NON-CHARITABLE PURPOSE TRUSTS

These trusts are sometimes called trusts of imperfect obligation because there is no one to enforce them.

The general rule is that for a trust to be valid it must have a human beneficiary by whom or for whom the trust can be enforced, *Morice v. Bishop of Durham* (1804).

A leading case on purpose trusts is *Re Astor S.T.* (1952). In that case a trust for "the maintenance of good understanding between nations and the preservation and integrity of newspapers" was held invalid on the ground not only that it was insufficiently certain but also that there was no human beneficiary.

There are exceptions to this rule and there are also purpose trusts which are deemed to have human beneficiaries.

Charitable trusts

Where the purpose of the trust is charitable then in spite of lacking a human beneficiary the trust will be valid. Such a trust can always be enforced by the Attorney-General. (See Chap. 11.)

The Anomalous cases—(the only real exceptions)

These cases were decided before *Re Astor S.T.* (1952). They have not been overruled by that case but they are unlikely to be extended.

In order to succeed the trust must be sufficiently certain and confined in duration to the perpetuity period. The perpetuity period is a life in being (a human life, not that of a cat, see *Re Kelly* (1932), though a royal lives clause has been permitted *Re Khoo Cheng Teow* (1932)), and 21 years. Where the testator does not specify a perpetuity period the court will normally confine the duration of the gift to 21 years as there will be no relevant life in being. The wait and see period does not apply to purpose trusts, section 15(4) of the Perpetuities and Accumulations Act 1964.

1. Trusts for specific animals. In *Pettingall v. Pettingall* (1842) a trust of £50 to look after the testator's favourite mare was upheld. A gift of £750 p.a. for the period of 50 years to maintain the testator's horses, ponies and hounds "if they should so long live" was upheld in *Re Dean* (1889) even though it offended the perpetuity rule.

2. Trusts for tombs and monuments. In *Pirbright v. Salwey* (1896) £800 was given to the rector of the parish to use the income, for so long as the law permitted, for the upkeep of a grave. It was upheld for 21 years. This case was followed in *Re Hooper* (1932), another case concerning the upkeep of family tombs and monuments.

The importance of confining the duration of the gift to the perpetuity period is illustrated by *Mussett v. Bingle* (1876). £300 was left to erect a monument to the first husband of the testator's wife and a further £200 for its upkeep in perpetuity. The first part of the gift was valid as it was assumed that the monument would be erected within the perpetuity period. The gift of £200 was invalid as it rendered the money inalienable for ever.

The importance of the gift being sufficiently certain is illustrated in *Re Endacott* (1960) (a case decided after *Re Astor* (1952) showing a hardening of the courts' attitude to the anomalous cases). A residuary gift of £20,000 given by the testator to the North Tawton Parish Council for the purpose of providing "some useful memorial to myself" failed because the words "some useful memorial" were too vague. The court does not like large sums of money being tied up for capricious purposes. See *Brown v. Burdett* (1822) and *McCaig v. Glasgow University* (1907). The Law Reform Committee in 1955 had suggested £1,000 would be a reasonable maximum for a tomb or memorial.

3. Trusts for masses. A trust for the saying of masses for a private individual was held valid, in *Bourne v. Keane* (1919).

4. Trusts for fox-hunting. Such a trust was held to be valid in
Re Thompson (1934).

Purpose trusts which are really for ascertainable individuals

If, "though expressed as a purpose, (the trust) is directly or indirectly for the benefit of an individual or individuals" then it will be
upheld. This quotation comes from *Re Denley* (1969) where there
was a trust of land given for the purpose of a sports ground for use
by the employees of a company and others. Clearly the sports
ground would benefit the employees. The trust being sufficiently
certain and confined in duration to the perpetuity period was therefore valid.

Unincorporated associations

In *Conservative and Unionist Central Office v. Burrell* (1982) an unincorporated association was said to exist where (1) two or more persons are bound together (2) for one or more common purposes (3)
by mutual undertakings, each having mutual duties and obligations
(4) in an organisation which has rules identifying in whom control
of the organisation and its funds is vested and (5) which can be
joined or left at will.

The main problem about gifts to an unincorporated association
is that it does not have a distinct legal entity, as an individual or a
corporation does, which can hold the property.

A gift to an unincorporated association can be construed in four
different ways.

(a) As a gift to present members of the association at the date
of the gift as joint tenants or tenants in common. The members
could if they wanted divide the property between themselves each
taking a share. This was the construction put upon a gift in *Cocks
v. Manners* (1871) where a testator left a share of his residue to the
Dominican Convent at Carisbrooke "payable to the superior for
the time being." If the gift were construed as including future
members, it would be void for perpetuity as the capital would be
tied up indefinitely and the present members would not be able to
dispose of it as they saw fit. It is possible that since the Perpetuities
and Accumulations Act 1964 the gift will not fail completely for
perpetuity but will be valid for those future members ascertained
within the perpetuity period, the others being excluded.

(b) As a gift to trustees or other proper officers of the committee for the purposes of the association. On this construction the
gift would fail for lack of a human beneficiary. In *Leahy v.
Att.-Gen. (New South Wales)* (1959) a gift of a sheep station for

"such order of nuns of the Catholic Church or the Christian brothers as my trustees shall select" was held not to be a gift for individual members of the order. In addition as the capital could not be spent, but only the income, as a private trust it was void for perpetuity.

(c) As a gift to the members of the association at the date of the gift, not as joint tenants, but subject to their contractual rights and liabilities towards one another as members of the association. The gift is deemed to be an accretion to the funds of the association. A member who leaves the association, by death or resignation, will, in the absence of any rules to the contrary, have no claim to the property, *Neville Estates v. Madden* (1962). In *Re Rechers Will Trusts* (1972) there was a gift to the Anti-Vivisection Society. The Society had a constitution under which control of any property was given to the members. They could band together and share out the property so that in effect they were the human beneficiaries. There was no restriction on the disposition of the capital of the fund so there was no problem about about perpetuity.

This approach was taken a step further in *Re Lipinski's Will Trust* (1976). A testator left part of his residuary estate to the Hull Judeans (Maccabi) Association "to be used solely in the work of constructing the new buildings for the association and for improvements to the said building." In other words the testator had clearly spelt out how he wished the money to be used. Nevertheless following *Re Denley* it was held that the gift was not really for a purpose but for the benefit of the Hull Judeans, ascertainable beneficiaries. Because according to the constitution of the association the members could if they wished alter the purpose for which the money could be used and, as in *Re Recher*, could divide the money between themselves, the trust was held valid. Where, however, the members of the association have no control of the funds the trust will fail. In *Re Grants Will Trusts* (1980) there was a trust for the purposes of the Chertsey Labour Party Headquarters. The members did not control the property nor could they change their constitution to enable them to do so as it was subject to the approval of an outside body, the National Executive Committee. The trust was void for perpetuity as there could be no disposition of the capital.

Nor could the *Denley* approach save a trust "for the benefit of any or all or some of the inhabitants of the County of West Yorkshire." The capital and income had to be applied well within the perpetuity period but the trust failed for want of ascertainable beneficiaries. The large class of potential beneficiaries made the trust unworkable. (*R. v. District Auditor, ex p. West Yorkshire Metropolitan County Council* (1986)).

(d) As a gift to members of the association imposing on them a mandate to apply the property for the purposes of the association. This is possible for a gift *inter vivos* but not a testamentary disposition. So far its use has not been fully explored but see *Conservative and Unionist Central Office v. Burrell (Inspector of Taxes)* (1982).

Powers

If the gift is drafted as a power rather than a trust, it can be perfectly valid even though there is no human beneficiary for there is no question of anyone being forced to exercise a power. In *Re Shaw* (1957) a gift by George Bernard Shaw for researching into the advantages of a new 40-letter alphabet failed as a trust but Harman J. indicated that it would succeed as a power. However, it would have to be drafted as a power in the first place. "We do not think a valid power is to be spelt out of an invalid trust."

---

11. CHARITABLE TRUSTS

Trusts which are for purposes beneficial to the community will be enforceable if they are considered to be charitable. The trustees may be individuals but more often are a corporate body.

Charities are supervised by the Charity Commission, Charities Act 1960. Stronger investigative powers have been given to the Commission by the Charities Act 1992.

ADVANTAGES OF CHARITABLE STATUS

1. Perpetuity. A gift must vest in a charity within the perpetuity period. Once so vested, however, a gift over to another charity can occur outside the perpetuity period; the vesting being for charitable purposes it does not matter that the actual charity is changed subsequently, *Christ's Hospital v. Grainger* (1849).

A charity is not subject to the rule against inalienability. Capital may be tied up indefinitely.

2. Certainty. Provided that the donor has shown a clear intention that the property be applied for charitable purposes it does not matter that he fails to choose a specific named charity. The court will draw up a scheme for division of the property to charities. Thus in *Moggridge v. Thackwell* (1803) the testatrix left her residuary property to a trustee to dispose of to charities as he thought fit. She recommended clergymen with large families and good character. The trustee predeceased the testatrix and the next-of-kin claimed the property. The court held that the property be applied exclusively to charity, even though the testatrix had not specified particular charitable objects.

3. Taxation. The main advantage of charitable status is the privileged tax position. A charity does not pay tax on income that is applied solely for charitable purposes, although in the case of a trade carried on by a charity the profits from the trade are only non-taxable if the trade is exercised in the course of the actual carrying out of a primary purpose of the charity or the work is mainly carried out by the beneficiaries of the charity, section 505(1) (e) of the Income and Corporation Taxes Act 1988. Where money is paid to charities under a covenant capable of exceeding 3 years the charity can claim the tax back, section 347A(7) of the I.C.T.A. 1988. There are also exemptions for gifts made to charities from Inheritance Tax, section 23 Inheritance Tax Act 1984, and there is no Capital Gains Tax on a gain made by a charity that is applied solely for charitable purposes, section 256(1) Taxation of Chargeable Gains Act 1992. All charities are entitled to 80 per cent council tax relief where land is occupied by or used by a charity and wholly or mainly used for charitable purposes. Further relief is at the discretion of the local authority.

ESSENTIALS OF A CHARITY

Charitable nature and public benefit

Trusts must both be of a charitable nature and have a sufficient public benefit if they are to qualify as charitable trusts. There is no legal definition of a charity. It has been said that "there is no limit to the number and diversity of ways in which man will seek to benefit his fellow men," *I.R.C. v. Baddeley* (H.L., 1955). The Nathan Committee Report held that a strict definition was neither possible nor desirable.

The statute of Elizabeth I, the Charitable Uses Act 1601, set out in the preamble a list of charitable objects. This preamble was finally repealed by the Charities Act 1960 but it is still used as a

guide by the courts. The best summary of these charitable purposes
is in Lord Macnaghten's speech in *Commissioners of Income Tax v.
Pemsel* (H.L., 1891). He divided charities into four main heads:
  (a) trusts for the relief of poverty;
  (b) trusts for the advancement of religion;
  (c) trusts for the advancement of education; and
  (d) trusts for other purposes beneficial to the community not fal-
      ling under any of the preceding heads.

1. Trusts for the relief of poverty. In *Re Coulhurst* (1951)
Evershed M.R. said "Poverty does not mean destitution; it is a word
of wide and somewhat indefinite import; it may not be unfairly
paraphrased for present purpose as meaning persons who have to
'go short' in the ordinary acceptance of that term, due regard being
had to their status in life and so forth." The case upheld as charitable a gift to be applied for widows and orphaned children of
deceased officers of Coutts & Company's Bank.

In the 1601 preamble the wording was trusts for the relief of
aged, impotent and poor people. These words have been interpreted disjunctively so that a trust for the relief of the aged will be
valid even where the aged are not also impotent and/or poor.
Impotent means handicapped. In *Re Lewis* (1955) a gift of £100 cash
to 10 blind girls and 10 blind boys in Tottenham was held valid
even though the gift was not restricted to the poor impotent. However, the gift must be for the *relief* of the aged or impotent; "a gift
of money to the aged millionaires of Mayfair would not relieve a
need of theirs as aged persons," *Joseph Rowntree Memorial Trust Housing Association Ltd v. Att.-Gen.* (1983). In that case the provision of
special accommodation relieved a particular need of the elderly of
limited means, even though the elderly were required to contribute
towards the cost of the scheme.

A gift will not be for the relief of poverty if it can benefit the
rich as well as the poor. In *Re Sander's W.T.* (1954) a gift for the
working classes, some of whom might be well off, was held not to
be charitable, although in *Re Njyazi's W.T.* (1978), a case described
as "desperately near the borderline," the construction of a working
men's hostel in Famagusta was held charitable. In an earlier case
Re Gwyon (1930) a gift to provide knickers for the boys of Farnham
failed on the ground that the rich too could benefit from the gift.

Under all four charitable heads there must be an element of
public benefit although in the case of poverty the public need not
be a very large class. A trust for the relief of poverty among specified persons is not charitable but a trust to relieve poverty amongst

needy relatives is, *Re Scarisbrick* (1951) as is a trust for poor employees, *Dingle v. Turner* (H.L., 1972). The Goodman Report (1976) recommended the statutory repeal of *Dingle v. Turner*.

2. Trusts for the advancement of education. The 1601 preamble was for the maintenance of " . . . schools of learning, free schools and scholars in universities." Education is no longer restricted to formal education in the classroom but there must be some element of instruction or improvement. In the *Incorporated Council of Law Reporting for England and Wales v. Att.-Gen.* (1972) the publication of law reports was held to be charitable because its purpose was beneficial to the community as it furthered the development and administration of law. It was also education as law reports were essential material for the study of law. On the other hand a gift which merely tends to the increase of knowledge without any teaching or education is not charitable. (*Re Shaw* (1957) G. B. Shaw's gift for a 40-letter alphabet was held not to be charitable.)

Gifts which have been upheld as charitable have included trusts to encourage and advance choral singing in London, *Royal Choral Society v. I.R.C.* (1943), to ensure the spread of knowledge and appreciation of Delius, (*Re Delius* (1957)—had he been a lesser-known composer the gift might not have been held to be charitable), to erect and endow the Shakespeare Memorial National Theatre with the object of performing Shakespeare's plays, reviving English classical drama, and stimulating the art of acting, *Re Shakespeare's Memorial Trust* (1923). Mrs Shaw's will, unlike her husband's, was upheld as a valid charitable trust; it provided for the encouragement and advancement of self-control, oratory, deportment and the art of personal contact in Ireland, *Re Shaw's W.T.* (1952). More recently a gift for the furtherance of the Wilton Park project (a conference centre for discussion of matters of international importance) was upheld as a charitable trust, in *Re Koeppler Will Trusts* (C.A., 1985).

Gifts which have failed as charitable trusts have included a bequest to found a college to train mediums, *Re Hummeltenberg* (1923) and a gift of the testator's study and its contents to found a museum. Expert opinion was unanimous in considering that the collection had no artistic merit. No useful object was served in foisting on the public a "mass of junk," *Re Pinion* (1965).

Trusts to advance sports as such are not charitable, *Re Nottage* (1895) (a trust to provide a cup for yachting). But if the sports are at a school, then they will be a part of the education and so charitable. In *Re Mariette* (1915) there was a valid charitable trust to provide Eton Fives Courts and Squash Courts at Aldenham School and a prize for athletics. The sporting facilities do not have to be at a particular school. In *I.R.C. v. McMullen* (H.L., 1981) a trust to provide facilities for soccer at schools and universities in the United Kingdom was held to assist the physical education and development of the young.

There must be a genuine public benefit in educational trusts. The law is anxious that educational trusts should not be used as a tax-planning device to provide education for the wealthy at the expense of the taxpayer. Nor will it allow employers to gain commercial advantage by setting up educational trusts for the children of their employees.

This is illustrated by the case of *Oppenheim v. Tobacco Securities Trust Co. Ltd* (H.L., 1951). Money was given to provide education for the children of employees of the British American Tobacco Corporation and its subsidiaries. The number of employees exceeded 110,000. It was held that even with these large numbers the personal nexus between the employers and employees meant that there was not a sufficient public benefit. Lord MacDermott dissented. He considered that the public benefit question should be one of degree depending on the facts of the particular case. In a later much-criticised case, *Re Koettgen's W.T.* (1954), a trust for promotion of commercial education amongst those who could not afford it, preference to be given to families of employees of a particular company of up to a maximum of 75 per cent of the income of the fund, was upheld as charitable. The gift was held to be primarily for the public, a mere preference being given to employee's families.

The poor relatives anomaly, which allows as charitable a gift for the relief of *poverty* amongst the testator's relatives, will not be extended to the *education* of the testator's poor relatives, *Re Compton* (1945).

3. Trusts for the advancement of religion. Religion is not restricted to the Christian religion, but it must have elements of faith and worship. In *Re Watson* (1973) a trust was upheld for the continuation of the work of God through the publication of the tracts of a certain Hobbs, a leading member of a very small Christian sect. Expert evidence had shown that the works were worthless. But in *Re South Place Ethical Society* (1980) the study of ethical and rational principles was held not to be religious though it was charitable under the head of education.

The Goodman Report (1976) has stated that account must be taken of the ethnic minorities and that the advancement of all religions, whether monotheistic or not, should be capable of existing as a charitable trust.

There must, of course, be a sufficient element of public benefit. In *Gilmour v. Coats* (H.L., 1949) a gift to an enclosed contemplative order of nuns failed. The nuns prayed for the world but the court held that prayer is "manifestly not susceptible of proof." A gift for masses for the dead has been held to have sufficient public benefit for the mass is part of a public ritual, *Re Hetherington* (1989). And in *Neville Estates v. Madden* (1962) a gift was upheld for the benefit of a synagogue in Catford. It was restricted to members of the Jewish faith but they were also members of the public. The court considered that as the congregation went out into the world there was sufficient public benefit. In *Re Le Cren Clarke deceased* (1996) the testatrix left her residuary estate for the spiritual work of a group to which she had belonged. The group's primary work was held to be a charitable gift notwithstanding that a subsidiary part of the work was private services which were not charitable.

4. Other purposes beneficial to the community. This is a vague heading but covers matters within the spirit of the 1601 statute. Examples include a gift for a Fire Brigade, *Re Wokingham Fire Brigade Trusts* (1951), gifts for the increased efficiency or morale of the army, *Re Good* (1905), gifts for the promotion of industry, commerce and art, *Crystal Palace Trustees v. Minister of Town & Country Planning* (1950).

Gifts for sport have not been upheld unless they are for sport within schools or the army, *Re Gray* (1925). Thus in *I.R.C. v. Glasgow Police Athletic Association* (1953) the association was deemed to be a sports club for members not a charity.

Trusts for orphans or orphanages have been upheld as charitable apart from the much-criticised case of *Re Cole* (1958) where a trust for the general welfare of children, both deprived and delinquent, in a home maintained by a local authority failed under this head.

Trusts for specific animals are not charitable but trusts for animals generally will be upheld if they promote and encourage human kindness, *Re Wedgewood* (1915). However, in *National Anti-Vivisection Society v. I.R.C.* (H.L., 1948) where money was given to further the cause of anti-vivisection the court held that the moral benefit resulting to mankind was outweighed by the detriment which would be suffered by medical research if experiments were not allowed on live animals.

The above case also failed because it had a political element. It sought to promote legislation to change the law which allowed vivisection. For the same reason in *McGovern v. Att.-Gen.* (1982) Amnesty International was held non-charitable. Only if the political element is incidental will it not be rejected by the courts. The Charity Commissioners have issued guidelines on political activity which are in many ways tighter than *McGovern*. Charities dealing with poverty, for instance, are not allowed to campaign against the social and economic causes of poverty.

Recreational charities have caused problems. In *Re Scowcroft* (1898) the maintenance of a village club and reading room "to be used for the furtherance of conservative principles and religious and mental improvement" was held charitable. In *I.R.C. v. Baddeley* (1955) a controversy arose over the stamp duty on a conveyance of land. If the trust was charitable no stamp duty would be payable. The trust was for the promotion of the religious, social and physical wellbeing of the Methodists of West Ham and Leyton. It failed on two grounds; first social purposes were not charitable; secondly there was not sufficient public benefit.

This decision led to the passing of the Recreational Charities Act 1958 which stated that it is charitable to provide, or assist in the provisions of, facilities for recreation or other leisure-time occupation, if the facilities are provided in the interests of social welfare. Social welfare is satisfied if (1) the facilities are provided with the object of improving the conditions of life for the persons for whom the facilities are primarily intended, and (2) *either* (a) persons have need of these facilities by reason of youth, age, infirmity or disablement, poverty or social and economic circumstances; or (b) the facilities are to be available to the members or female members of the public at large. In *Guild v. IRC* (1992) the House of Lords rejected the argument that "in the interests of social welfare" meant that the intended recipients must be in some form of need. A recreational facility could be charitable if it improved the conditions of life for all members of the community.

Subject to the social welfare test the following are specifically included as charitable under the Act:

> "facilities at village halls, community centres and women's institutes, and to the provision and maintenance of grounds and buildings to be used for purposes of recreation and leisure-time occupation."

It should be noted, however, that even under the Act the trust must be for the public benefit. The *Baddeley* case would probably still fail because it was restricted to a class within a class; Methodists in the West Ham and Leyton area.

Exclusively charitable

Besides being of a charitable nature and having a public benefit the gift must be exclusively charitable.

Where a gift is given for a number of specific purposes it will not be a valid charitable trust unless all the purposes are charitable. In *Morice v. Bishop of Durham* (1805) a gift for benevolent purposes was held not to be exclusively charitable. Phrases such as charitable or benevolent, charitable or deserving and so on have been held to lack the exclusively charitable requirement. A gift, however, "for educational or charitable or religious purposes" was held valid in *Re Ward* (1941) because each of the heads was exclusively charitable.

Phrases such as "charitable *and* deserving" or "charitable and benevolent" are sometimes upheld as wholly charitable by construing the meaning as those charitable objects which are also benevolent or deserving. It is explained in the textbooks as using the words "and" or "or" conjunctively. Where the words import alternatives then they are said to be used disjunctively.

There are some situations where the rule that the gift must be exclusively charitable will not apply.

1. Apportionment. If an executor or trustee is directed to divide property between charitable and non-charitable objects the trust will not wholly fail. In default of appointment by the executor the court will divide the fund equally and the trust will be valid as to the charitable half.

2. Ancillary purpose. It does not matter if a trust for charitable purposes incidentally benefits objects which are not charitable. In *Royal College of Surgeons v. National Provincial Bank* (H.L., 1952) the object of the trust was to found an institution for the promotion of practice in surgery. The court brushed aside an objection that it also benefited professional surgeons. And in *Re Coxen* (1948) the fact that a testator, who had given a large sum of money for the benefit of orthopaedic hospitals, directed that £100 could be used for a dinner for the trustees, when they met to carry out the business of the trust, did not stop the trust from being exclusively charitable. A recent case on ancillary purpose is *Att.-Gen. v. Ross* (1985). The student union of the Polytechnic of North London was necessarily charitable being an integral part of the polytechnic which is itself a charity. The fact that the student union acted in an *ultra vires* and non-charitable fashion could not deprive it of that status, nor could the fact that in furthering education it indulged in ancillary political activities permitted by its constitution.

The position is different, however, where there is a gift to an institution whose *purposes* although mainly charitable include non-charitable purposes. Two cases illustrate this. In *Oxford Group v. I.R.C.* (1949) the main object of the Group, an incorporated body, was the advancement of religion. Another of its objects was the maintenance, support, development and assistance of the Group in every way. In *Ellis v. I.R.C.* (1949) property was conveyed for use generally in such manner for the promotion and aiding of the work of the Roman Catholic Church as the trustees with the consent of the bishop might prescribe. In both these decisions the court said that the purpose was not exclusively charitable. The non-charitable purpose existed in its own right and this was sufficient to invalidate the charitable status.

The public displeasure aroused by these cases resulted in Parliament passing the Charitable Trust (Validation) Act 1954. It is of very limited ambit. Where a trust came into operation before December 16, 1952, and the purposes are such that the property whilst it could be applied exclusively for charity could also benefit non-charitable purposes then from July 30, 1954, onwards the gift will be construed as if the provision had required the property to be held only for charitable purposes.

3. The locality cases. Trusts for the benefit of my country England, *Re Smith* (1932) and for a particular locality have been interpreted by the courts as limited to charitable purposes. But they cannot do so where the donor has spelt out the purposes some of which are non-charitable. So a bequest to be used for a public purpose in a Scottish village failed as a charitable trust, *Houston v. Burns* (H.L., 1918).

4. Gifts to officials. A gift to someone by virtue of his office with no purpose specified will be deemed to be given to him for charitable purposes only, assuming that the duties of the office are charitable. A gift to a vicar and churchwardens of a named parish to be applied as in their sole discretion they thought fit, *Re Garrard* (1907) or to a bishop on similar terms, *Re Rumball* (1956) or a gift for any purposes in connection with the church which vicar and churchwardens might think fit, *Re Eastes* (1948), have all been held to be exclusively charitable. However, where words are added by the donor which show that the gift although given to a charitable corporation or official could be used for non-charitable purposes the gift will not be held charitable. Gifts given to a vicar "for parish work," *Farley v. Westminster Bank* (H.L., 1939), or "for parochial institutions and purposes," *Re Stratton* (1931) have failed because parish purposes are not synonymous with religion.

THE CY-PRES DOCTRINE

If a non-charitable trust is initially ineffective or subsequently fails there is a resulting trust to the settlor. In the case of a charitable trust the trust property can be applied for another charitable purpose as close as possible to the original trust. This is known as the doctrine of *cy-près*.

For the doctrine to apply two conditions must be fulfilled. The original purpose must be impossible or impractical and secondly the donor must have shown a paramount intention to benefit charity.

Impossibility

In *Att.-Gen. v. City of London* (1790) the trust included the advancement and propagation of the Christian religion among the infidels of Virginia. It was held that the purpose was at the time of the case impossible as there were no infidels in Virginia.

A creative use of *cy-près* occurred in *Re Lysaght* (1966). The testatrix provided funds to found medical scholarships to be run by the Royal College of Surgeons. One of the terms was that the awards were not to be made to Jews or Roman Catholics. The Royal College refused to accept the gift on these terms so it became impractical to carry out the trust. The court, therefore, deleted the religious discrimination clause.

The Charities Act 1960 has relaxed the requirement of impossibility. Section 13(1) provides that property may be applied *cy-près*:

(a) where the original purposes, in whole or in part—
   (i) have been as far as may be fulfilled; or
   (ii) cannot be carried out or not according to the directions given and to the spirit of the gift; or
(b) where the original purposes provide a use for part only of the property available by virtue of the gift; or
(c) where the property available by virtue of the gift and other property applicable for similar purposes can be more effectively used in conjunction, and to that end can suitably, regard being had to the spirit of the gift, be made applicable to common purposes; or
(d) where the original purposes were laid down by reference to an area which then was but has since ceased to be a unit for some other purpose, or by reference to a class of persons or to an area which has for any reason since ceased to be suitable, regard being had to the spirit of the gift, or to be practical in administering the gift; or

(e) where the original purposes, in whole or in part, have since they were laid down:
  (i) been adequately provided for by other means; or
  (ii) ceased, as being useless or harmful to the community or for other reasons, to be in law charitable; or
  (iii) ceased in any other way to provide a suitable and effective method of using the property available by virtue of the gift, regard being had to the spirit of the gift.

Subsections (a) and (e)(iii) were relied on in *Re Lepton's Charity* (1972). A will dated 1715 directed £3 p.a. to be paid to the minister and any surplus income to the poor. By 1970 the income had risen from £5 to £800. The court increased the stipend to £100 per annum.

In *Peggs v. Lamb* (1994) a scheme was authorised under (d) where a charitable purpose which was originally for the benefit of the freeman was enlarged to cover the inhabitants of the borough as a whole, the qualifying freemen having significantly declined in numbers.

A further modest relaxation is the Charities Act 1985. This Act only applies to small local charities, at least 50 years old, for the relief of poverty. Provided certain conditions are fulfilled the trustees, with the consent of the Charity Commissioners, can alter the objects of the trust if they consider them to be obsolete or lacking in usefulness, or impossible of achievement.

Paramount intention to benefit charity

1. Initial impossibility. Where the trust is impossible at the date of the gift the donor must have manifested a paramount intention to give to charity for the *cy-près* doctrine to apply. It is only if this intention can be found that it is considered fair to defeat those people who otherwise would be entitled to the property; (*i.e.* if it is a gift by will, those entitled to the residue or where it is a gift of residue those entitled on intestacy).

No such intention need be shown in the following circumstances:
(a) Under section 14 of the Charities Act 1960 where the donor has disclaimed or cannot be identified or found as where the money has been raised through collecting boxes, lotteries, competitions and so forth.
(b) Where the defunct charity is continued in another form, *e.g.* it has been amalgamated with another charity or has been reconstituted under new trusts; (see *Re Faraker* (1912): consolidation of local charities for the relief of the poor in Rotherhithe did not destroy original trusts).

(c) Where the gift is to a corporation with charitable objects which is dissolved if the gift was to the corporation *in trust for its objects* unless either that particular corporate trust was an essential prerequisite of the gift or the gift was a straight gift to the corporation, *Re Vernon's W.T.* (1972).

(d) Where the gift is to an unincorporated association established for charitable purposes and those charitable purposes continue to exist.

Re Finger's Will Trusts (1972) illustrates (c) and (d). There was a gift to the National Radium Commission, an unincorporated association, and to the National Council for Maternity and Child Welfare, an incorporated body. When the testatrix died both bodies had ceased to exist; the purposes of the National Radium Commission continued to exist and the gift was held to be a gift to those purposes. It did not matter that the trustee no longer existed. The gift to the incorporated body prima facie should have failed. It was a gift to that particular body not on trust for its purposes. The court, however, found on the particular facts of the case the testatrix had a paramount charitable intention and so the gift was applied *cy-près*.

There are no definitions of what amounts to a paramount charitable intent. It is difficult to establish such an intention where:

(a) the gift is to a particular charity which has been described accurately by the testator and has ceased to exist before his death, *Re Harwood* (1936). In that case a testatrix left £200 to the Wisbech Peace Society which had ceased to exist at her death;

(b) the testator had only one particular purpose in mind, such as to found a school at a particular place and that purpose cannot be carried out, *Re Wilson* (1913).

Indications of a paramount charitable intent occur where:

(a) the testator has made several gifts to charities especially where they are of a similar nature;

(b) the gift is to an institution which has never in fact existed. In *Re Harwood* as well as a gift to the Wisbech Peace Society there was a further gift to a society in Belfast which had never existed. This gift went *cy-près*.

It should be emphasised that these are only guidelines. The cases show little consistency in the court's approach.

2. Subsequent impossibility. Where the property has initially been held on a charitable trust which subsequently becomes impracticable or impossible there is no need to find a paramount charitable intent. The reason is that those who would otherwise have taken the property have grown accustomed to being without it. Indeed it may be difficult to trace them. The gift will, therefore, go *cy-près* unless there is an indication to the contrary by the donor. He may for instance have provided for a gift over on the failure of a particular body.

The time for deciding whether there is an initial failure is at the time of the gift. If the gift is possible at that time but, before it is available for the charity, it becomes impossible it still counts as a case of subsequent impossibility. In *Re Wright* (1954) the testatrix died in 1933 leaving her residuary estate to a tenant for life, the remainder to be used to found a house for convalescent and impecunious gentlewomen. By the time the life tenant died in 1942 it was impracticable to found the home. The court found that dedication to charity occurred in 1933 and so the gift could be applied *cy-près* without the need of finding any paramount charitable intent.

3. Straight gift to charitable institution which subsequently ceases to exist after the testator's death. In this case there is no trust so the doctrine of *cy-près* does not apply. Those entitled to the residue or on intestacy cannot claim because the institution was in existence at the testator's death. All the property of the dissolved institution passes to the Crown as *bona vacantia*. As a matter of grace the Crown will allow the legacy to be applied for other charitable purposes.

12. APPOINTMENT, RETIREMENT AND REMOVAL OF TRUSTEES

CAPACITY AND NUMBER

Generally any person who has the capacity to hold property can be a trustee.

A minor cannot be appointed a trustee nor can he hold a legal estate, section 20 of the Law of Property Act 1925. However, a minor can be a trustee of personal property held on a resulting, implied or constructive trust. In *Re Vinogradoff* (1935) a grandmother put War Loan stock into the names of herself and her granddaughter. The granddaughter was only four years old. It was held that there was no presumption of a gift in the child's favour so she was a trustee holding the property on a resulting trust for her grandmother.

Infancy is one of the grounds for removing a trustee and appointing another under section 36(1) of the Trustee Act 1925.

A corporation can be a trustee. Some corporations are known as trust corporations. These include the Public Trustee, the Treasury Solicitor, the Official Solicitor, certain charitable or public corporations and those corporations entitled to act as custodian trustees under the Public Trustee Act 1906.

In a trust or settlement of *land* made after 1925 the maximum permitted number of trustees is four. A minimum of two trustees is required to give a valid receipt except where the trustee is a trust corporation, section 27(2) of the Law of Property Act 1925 and section 18(1) of the Settled Land Act 1925.

In a trust of personal property one trustee can give a receipt for capital money and there is no limit on the number of trustees who can be appointed.

APPOINTMENT OF TRUSTEES

There is a general equitable principle that "Equity does not want for a trustee." This means that if a settlor has failed to appoint trustees, or if the appointed trustees refuse, or are unable, to act or have ceased to exist then the trust will not fail. There is an exception to this rule if the trust is conditional upon certain people acting as trustees, *Re Lysaght, Hill v. Royal College of Surgeons* (1966).

Initial trustees

The first trustees are generally appointed in the will or settlement. If a settlor fails to appoint trustees the property will revert to the settlor. If a testator fails to appoint trustees or they predecease him, the property will be held by the personal representatives. In both cases the property will be held on the terms of the trust or settlement.

Where one of the initial trustees dies the property vests in the survivor(s). When the last survivor dies the property vests in his personal representatives, subject to the trust, section 18 of the Trustee Act 1925.

Appointment of subsequent trustees

The settlor cannot appoint new trustees once the trust has been properly constituted unless there is an express power for him to do so. Although beneficiaries who are *sui juris* and entitled to the whole beneficial interest can terminate the trust under the rule in *Saunders v. Vautier* (1841) it seemed that before the commencement of the Trusts of Land and Appointment of Trustees Act 1996 they probably could not appoint a new trustee. In *Re Brockbank* (1948) the existing trustees were in disagreement with all the beneficiaries about who should be appointed a new trustee. The beneficiaries and retiring trustee applied to the court. The court held that the decision of the trustees should prevail over the wishes of the beneficiaries.

The 1996 Act reverses the effect of *Re Brockbank* and entitles the beneficiaries to appoint new trustees except where the power to appoint trustees is vested in someone nominated for the purpose in the trust instrument.

1. Express power of appointment. The trust instrument may confer an express power of appointment. Reliance, however, is usually placed on the wide statutory power. The trust instrument will often nominate those who should exercise that power.

2. The statutory power. Unless there is a contrary provision in the trust instrument section 36 of the Trustee Act 1925 provides that a *replacement* trustee may be appointed where:

(a) the trustee is dead including a person appointed in a will who dies before the testator;
(b) the trustee remains outside the United Kingdom for a continuous period exceeding 12 months. This ground is often expressly excluded where for tax reasons all the trust property is outside the United Kingdom;
(c) the trustee wants to retire;
(d) the trustee refuses to act or disclaims before accepting office;
(e) the trustee is unfit to act as where he is bankrupt;
(f) the trustee is incapable of acting. This includes physical and mental illness, (governed by the Mental Health Act 1983) old age and, in the case of a corporation, dissolution;
(g) the trustee of an implied, resulting or constructive trust is an infant; or
(h) the trustee is removed under a power in the trust instrument.

Section 36(6) of the Trustee Act 1925 provides that *additional* trustees may be appointed in any case where there are not more than three trustees, or a trust corporation.

An appointment under section 36(1) or (6) must be made in writing and should be made by:

(a) the persons nominated in the trust instrument for the purpose of appointing new trustees or failing such a person;
(b) all the beneficiaries who are of full age and capacity and

together absolutely entitled to the trust property. The rules
are explained below, if the beneficiaries do not exercise their
rights then;

(c) the surviving or continuing trustees. The term trustees
includes those who are retiring or refusing to act but not
those being removed against their will. If such trustees are
dead then;

(d) the personal representatives of the last surviving or continuing trustee. This, of course, has no application where an *additional* trustee is being appointed;

(e) the court under section 41 of the Trustee Act 1925 (discretionary power on the failure of (a), (b), (c) and (d) above).

Where a trustee is being replaced, anyone can be appointed a
new trustee including the appointor himself. He cannot, however,
appoint himself when an *additional* trustee is being appointed under
section 36(6).

In trusts of both real and personal property it does not matter if
the number of trustees is increased by the appointment. Nor is there
any need to fill up the numbers of trustees where they exceed two.
In trusts of personal property where only one trustee was originally
appointed there is no obligation to appoint more than one trustee
and a trustee may be discharged leaving only one trustee. In other
cases there must be left either two or more trustees or a trust corporation to perform the trust, section 37 of the Trustee Act 1925.

If the trust property is land then the maximum number of
trustees is always four and the minimum is two.

**3. Directions under The Trusts of Land and Appointment of
Trustees Act 1996.** The beneficiaries have power to give a written
direction to a trustee or trustees for the time being, including
anyone being directed to retire at the same time, to appoint as a
trustee or trustees the person or persons specified in the direction.
If there are no trustees then the direction has to be given to the
personal representative of the last person who was a trustee.

The power can be exercised only where there is no person nominated for the purpose of appointing new trustees by the trust instrument. In addition the beneficiaries must be of full age and capacity
and taken together absolutely entitled to the trust property.

Where a new trustee is needed because of the mental disorder
of an existing trustee, and there is no-one entitled and willing and
able to appoint a trustee in place of him, under section 31 of the
Trustee Act 1925, the beneficiaries may give the written direction
to a Receiver of the Trustee, an Attorney with an Enduring Power

or a person authorised by the authority having jurisdiction under Part VII of the Mental Health Act 1983.

Section 31 of the Trustee Act provides that the following may appoint new trustees:

(a) the person or persons nominated for the purpose of appointing new trustees by the instrument, if any, creating the trusts;

(b) if there is no such person, or no such person able and willingly to act, then the surviving or continuing trustees for the time being, or the personal representatives of the last surviving or continuing trustees.

The recipient must appoint by writing the person or persons specified in the direction to be a trustee or trustees in place of the incapable trustee. More than one trustee may be necessary where the sole remaining trustee is unable to appoint a new trustee.

4. Appointment by the court.   (a) Under section 41 of the Trustee Act 1925 the court has a wide power to appoint new trustees "either in substitution for or in addition to any existing trustee or trustees, or although there is no existing trustee." In particular the court may appoint a new trustee where any existing trustee is mentally unfit to act, or is a bankrupt, or being a corporation, is in liquidation or has been dissolved. An order can be made on the application of a trustee or beneficiary, section 58 of the Trustee Act 1925.

The court will not appoint a person excluded from being a trustee under section 36(1) (*e.g.* a person under a mental disability or living abroad) and it will be reluctant to appoint a beneficiary because of a possible conflict in interest. In *Re Tempest* (1866) Turner L.J. stated that the court should have regard to the wishes of the person by whom the trust was created, the interests, even if conflicting, of all the beneficiaries and the efficient administration of the trust.

(b) Under the Judicial Trustee Act 1896 the settlor, or a trustee, or a beneficiary can make an application for the appointment of a trustee by the court. The court can appoint any fit person nominated in the application or an official of the court, to act solely or jointly with other trustees. A Judicial Trustee is a paid officer of the court and subject to its control and supervision.

(c) Under the Public Trustee Act 1906 on an application by a trustee or beneficiary the court has power to appoint the Public Trustee as a new or additional trustee.

VESTING OF TRUST PROPERTY

The trust property has to be vested in the new trustees. Section 40 of the Trustee Act 1925 provides that where the trustee is appointed by deed a vesting declaration in the deed will vest the property in the trustees, and such a declaration may be implied subject to any provision in the deed to the contrary. There is no need for an express conveyance or assignment.

This section does not apply to:

(a) land mortgaged to secure money subject to a trust;
(b) land held under a lease which contains a covenant against assignment without consent unless the consent has been obtained before the execution of the deed,
(c) stocks and shares.

Exception (a) keeps the trusts off the title. Trustees who lend money on mortgage do not disclose the existence of the trust. On the appointment of new trustees there must be a separate transfer of the mortgage. The borrower will thus know to whom to repay the money without inspecting the trust instrument and deeds of appointment.

Exception (b) prevents the appointment causing an inadvertent breach of covenant against assigning.

Exception (c) recognises that the legal title to shares can only be effected by registration with the relevant company.

The court has a power to vest trust property in the new trustees where there is any difficulty.

DETERMINATION OF THE TRUSTEESHIP

Disclaimer

A trustee is not bound to accept the onerous duties of a trustee just because he is named in a trust instrument or because he has previously agreed to be a trustee. He must disclaim before he has done any act indicating acceptance. He cannot disclaim part only of the trust, *Re Lord Fullertons Contract* (1896).

When disclaiming a trust it is advisable, though not essential, to do so by deed.

If the trustee disclaiming is the sole trustee the trust property will revert to the settlor or his personal representatives upon trust. If there are other trustees the property will remain with them.

Retirement

Under section 39 of the Trustee Act a trustee may retire by deed from the trust provided that either a trust corporation or two trustees will be left after his retirement and his co-trustees and the person, if any, entitled to appoint new trustees, consent by deed. Where the Public Trustee has been appointed a co-trustee can retire without these conditions being fulfilled.

The deed of retirement will normally contain a declaration by the retiring and continuing trustee vesting the property in the continuing trustees, and one will be implied unless there is a contrary intention. Mortgages, leases with a covenant against assignment, and stocks and shares will have to be transferred separately as on appointment, section 40(2), (3) Trustee Act 1925.

Replacement

A trustee may retire under section 36(1) on being replaced by someone else.

Removal

A trustee can be removed on the grounds set out in section 36(1) (see statutory grounds for appointing a replacement trustee). The court also has an inherent jurisdiction to remove a trustee. In *Letterstedt v. Broers* (1884) a beneficiary made several allegations of misconduct against the trustees and asked for their removal. He succeeded. It was held that the duty of the court was to ensure the proper execution of the trust. Even if the facts are disputed, or the trustees can disprove the allegations, they may be removed if there is disharmony. The welfare of the beneficiary is paramount.

On the other hand the court can consider the expense to the trust of a change of trustees and decide against removal even where there has been a minor breach of trust, *Re Wrightson* (1908).

A trustee who sets up a rival business may not be in breach of trust but the conflict of interest would be a ground for his removal, *Moore v. M'Glynn* (1896).

Direction by beneficiary to retire

Beneficiaries who are unanimous, of full age and capacity and between them entitled to the whole beneficial interest, may direct the retirement of a trustee provided there is no person alive at the time of the direction nominated in the trust instrument for appointing new trustees.

The conditions for the retirement of a trustee are:
(1) a written direction must be given to him
(2) reasonable arrangements must be made for the protection of any rights of his in connection with the trust

(3) on his retirement there must remain a trust corporation or at least two trustees

(4) a new trustee must be appointed on his retirement or if no such appointment is to be made the continuing trustees must consent by deed to his retirement

(5) the retiring trustee must execute a deed of discharge. (He has the ability to defer the deed until reasonable arrangements for his protection have been made)

(6) the retiring and continuing trustees and any new trustee must do anything necessary to vest the trust property in the continuing and new trustees.

A trustee who is directed to retire may have rights in respect of the trust property. He might have rights of reimbursement or indemnity for expenses incurred in relation to the trust and he may need to take action to ensure that he can enforce those rights. He may need to guard himself against taxation liabilities for which he could be held responsible after his retirement or he may have incurred contractual liabilities to third parties in dealing with the trust property.

The Act therefore provides that he shall only be under an obligation to execute a deed of retirement after reasonable arrangements have been made for the protection of any rights of his in connection with the trust.

Rules on Directions for appointment and Retirement of Trustees

A direction can be given jointly by all of the beneficiaries, or by each of them separately, or by some of them separately and some of them jointly. However, where more than one direction is given, each must specify for an appointment or retirement the same person or persons.

A beneficiary may withdraw in writing a direction which has been given provided that it has not been complied with. This power exists whether the direction was given jointly or singly. The purpose of the section is to deal with the risk of undue influence.

The trustee appointed will have the same powers as if he had been appointed a trustee by the instrument creating the trust.

Directions for the appointment of new trustees of land and of new trustees of the proceeds of sale of land must specify the same persons for both. If there are already trustees of any trust of the proceeds of sale of the land the directions must specify for appointment the same trustees for the land.

13. DUTIES

The duties of a trustee are extremely onerous. They have to be carried out with the utmost diligence. Otherwise the trustees are liable for breach of trust. The duty of the trustee is to act in the best interests of the trust even where this might conflict with his personal code of honour. In *Buttle v. Saunders* (1950) the trustees who had previously resisted a temptation to gazump were held bound to accept a higher offer. A trustee also has to exercise discretions. The standard is the care a prudent man of business would exercise in managing his own affairs, *Speight v. Gaunt* (1883).

On accepting the trust the trustee should:

(a) make himself familiar with the terms of the trust, the contents of any documents handed to him as trustee and the assets of the trust;

(b) ensure that the trust property is vested in him and his co-trustees;

(c) consider the investments.

If the trustee is replacing another trustee he should ensure that there have been no past breaches of trust for which he might be made jointly liable.

The trust property

(a) The trustees ought to call in the trust property. Thus if part of the property is a loan due for repayment this should be called in because if it becomes statute-barred under the Limitation Act 1980 the trustees are personally liable, unless they can show that they have a well-founded belief that any enforcement action would be pointless, *Re Brogden* (1888).

(b) The trust property ought to be in the joint control of all the trustees. In *Lewis v. Nobbs* (1878) the trust property included bearer bonds half of which were in the sole control of each trustee. When one of the trustees went off with the half in his custody the other trustee was held liable.

Section 7 of the Trustee Act 1925 provides that (1) "securities to bearer" should, until sold, be deposited with a bank and (2) a trustee should not be liable for any loss resulting from such deposit. Section 21 enables trustees to deposit any trust documents with a bank or company which undertakes safe custody of deeds.

Investments

1. Express powers The trustees must invest the trust property wisely acting as a prudent man making investments "for the benefit

of other people for whom he felt morally bound to provide," *Learoyd
v. Whiteley* (1887). Trustees must obtain the best rate of return
available coupled with diversification of risks even where it is
against the political, social or moral views of some of the beneficiaries, *Cowan v. Scargill* (1984). Although charitable trustees can
exclude certain investments (*e.g.* in armaments) they cannot pursue
a complete policy of ethical investment as this would be financially
detrimental to the trust fund, *Harries v. Church Commissioners* (1992).

Originally the only authorised investments were mortgages, government funds and other investments authorised by the settlement.
Express powers of investment were often included in trusts but
they were restrictively construed. The Trustee Investment Act 1961
was passed to increase the range of authorised investments. As it
applied to trusts set up before as well as after the Act it greatly
enlarged the trustees' investment powers in many existing trusts.

When the Act was first passed it became less necessary for trusts
to contain express investment powers. Today with inflation they
are once again necessary as the trustee investment powers given
by the Act are unsatisfactory and are often detrimental to the trust.
Since *Re Harari's S.T.* (1949) the court has given a more liberal
interpretation to express powers of investment. In that case
trustees were given power to invest "in or upon such investments
as to them may seem fit." The judge held that the trustees were
not limited to the trustee range of investments. The words had
their natural and proper meaning.

However, even where such a wide power is given, the trustees
must act honestly and with reasonable prudence. They must not,
for instance, make loans on personal security, *Re Peczenik's S.T.*
(1964).

2. The Trustee Investment Act 1961. It was not until the
Trustee Investment Act 1961 that trustees were allowed to invest
in ordinary shares (equities) unless there was an express investment clause to that effect.

The Act divides investments into narrower- and wider-range
investments (see Schedule I). Narrower-range investments are sub-
divided into:

   (a) Narrower-range investments not requiring advice. Examples
       include Defence Bonds, National Savings Certificates,
       deposits in Trustee Savings Banks.
   (b) Narrower-range investments requiring advice. These include
       fixed-interest securities issued by the government or public
       authorities, debentures, local authority loans, building society
       deposits.

Part III of Schedule I permits wide-range investments where five conditions are met:

(a) the shares must be issued in the United Kingdom by a company incorporated in the United Kingdom;

(b) the company must have an issued and paid-up share-capital of at least one million pounds;

(c) the company should have paid a dividend on all its shares which ranked for dividend in each of the five years preceding the purchase;

(d) the shares must be quoted on a recognised stock exchange; and

(e) the shares must be fully paid up or required to be paid up within nine months of the date of issue.

Before an investment is made in the wider range the whole trust fund must be divided into two equal parts, the narrower range and the wider range. The trustees may rely on a written valuation made by a person reasonably believed to be qualified, section 5 of the Trustee Investment Act 1961.

If property is transferred from one half to the other there must be a compensating transfer, section 2. Subsequent additions to the trust fund must be divided between the two parts or dealt with by means of a compensating transfer in order to achieve equality. This does not apply if the addition accrues from property in one of the parts. For instance if there is a bonus issue of shares in the wider range the wider range will be entitled to retain the full increase.

Trustees are allowed to withdraw property from the trust fund in exercise of their powers of advancement and maintenance. There are no requirements to balance any withdrawal. However, if the withdrawal was solely from the narrower range it might adversely affect the balance and security of the trust fund and the trustees might then be held to have failed in their duty to act as prudent men of business.

The powers under the Trustee Investment Act are in addition to any powers of investment (or of postponing conversion) contained in the trust instrument. If trustees wish to invest under the Act as well as under the trust instrument they have to divide the funds into three: narrower-range investments, wider-range investments and special-range investments, which may include wider-range investments.

3. Jurisdiction of the court to vary powers of investment.

Application can be made to give or vary a special power of investment under the Variation of Trusts Act 1958 or section 57 of the

Trustee Act 1925. It used to be unusual for the courts to give a wider power than that given by the Trustee Investment Act. With inflation, however, it has become apparent that the investment provisions are out of date and often detrimental to the trust and in two recent cases *Mason v. Farbrother* (1983) and *Trustees of the British Museum v. Att.-Gen.* (1984) much wider powers of investment were given by the court to the trustees. See also *Steel v. Wellcome Trustees Ltd* (1988) where because of the size of the fund, the eminence of the trustees and the provisions for expert advice a variation was made giving trustees investment powers of a beneficial owner. There was no provision for narrow-range investments.

4. Investment in real property. (a) Mortgages. The Trustee Investment Act 1961 allows a trustee to lend money on mortgage on freehold land and leasehold property where the lease has at least 60 years left to run. It is possible that the pre-1961 rule that the investment must be a first legal mortgage still applies.

The trustees must exercise their discretion when lending money on mortgage even where it is authorised. Section 8 of the Trustee Act 1925 provides that no more than two-thirds of the value of the property should be lent on mortgage. The trustee should obtain a report as to the value of the property from a surveyor or valuer, employed independently of any owner of the property, and should make a loan only on the advice of such surveyor or valuer. If a proper mortgage turns out to provide insufficient security the trustees will not be liable for the loss. If it would have been a proper mortgage for a smaller amount then the trustee is liable only for the excess, section 9. If it is a wholly unauthorised mortgage then the trustee must bear the full loss. Under section 10 of the Trustee Act 1925 a tenant for life when selling freehold land, or leasehold with at least 500 years to run, may leave not more than two-thirds of the purchase price on mortgage. The same section provides that if certain conditions are fulfilled trustees can contract not to call in a mortgage for a period not exceeding seven years.

(b) Purchase of land. The Trustee Investment Act 1961 does not authorise trustees to purchase land. Under the Settled Land Act 1925 trust money can be invested in freehold land, or in leasehold property having 60 years left to run.

The Trusts of Land and Appointment of Trustees Act 1996 gives trustees of land, and trustees of the proceeds of land, power to purchase land in England and Wales. The power does not extend to purchasing land in other countries, but the trust instrument could authorise the purchase of foreign land.

The land may be purchased for occupation by the beneficiaries, for an investment or for any other reason. The power extends to the purchase of both freehold and leasehold interests. There is no requirement that the lease should have more than 60 years to run.

Under the law existing before the commencement of the 1996 Act, it was not clear whether the trustees had power to let beneficiaries occupy the land subject to the trust.

Although under the 1996 Act the trustees are given the powers of absolute owners without special provision, it might not be considered that letting beneficiaries into occupation was a proper exercise of the powers. The Act therefore specifically gives certain beneficiaries the right to occupy such land. This right may be restricted or excluded in certain circumstances.

It is only beneficiaries entitled to an interest in possession in the land who have a right to occupy. This ensures that beneficiaries of pension schemes will not qualify to occupy the land. Those with a purely monetary interest, such an annuitants, are excluded. So are those with a future or contingent interest.

However, not all such beneficiaries will be entitled to occupation. The purposes of the trust must include making the land available for the occupation of the particular beneficiary or for the occupation of beneficiaries of a class of which he is a member, or for beneficiaries generally. Alternatively, the land must be held by the trustees so as to be available for occupation. It does not have had to be acquired specifically for that purpose. A house might have been acquired for resale but subsequently the trustees might decide not to sell the property but to allow the beneficiary to reside there.

However, although a beneficiary might have a prima facie right to occupation, this can be excluded if the land is unavailable or unsuitable for occupation by him. An example of premises being unsuitable would be where a farm became available but the beneficiary had no farming experience or expertise.

Where two or more beneficiaries have a right to occupy the trustees have power to regulate the occupation. They may restrict or exclude the right of one or more to occupy the property. However, the trustees cannot exclude the rights of occupation of all the beneficiaries.

In exercising their power to exclude or restrict any beneficiary's right to occupancy, the trustees must not act unreasonably.

Where a beneficiary or beneficiaries have a right to occupy, the trustees may, not just at the beginning of the occupation, but from time to time, impose reasonable conditions. These conditions are not only for protecting the interests of those with competing rights, but also the interests of those beneficiaries who do not have a right to occupy.

When exercising their power to exclude or restrict the right to occupy or to impose conditions, the trustees must take into account, amongst other things:

(1) the intentions of those who created the trust
(2) the purpose for which the land is held
(3) the circumstances and wishes of each of the beneficiaries who has a right or whose right has been excluded or restricted to occupy the land.

Conditions imposed by the trustees may include an obligation to pay outgoings and rent in respect of the land and to asume any other obligation in respect of the land or to any other activity which is, or is proposed to be, conducted there.

Where a beneficiary's right to occupy land has been excluded or restricted under section 12, the trustees may impose conditions on any other beneficiary to make payments to him by way of compensation or to benefit him by forgoing any payments or other advantages to which that other beneficiary would otherwise be entitled.

The list of considerations which the Act specifies that trustees can impose in respect of the occupation of the land by a beneficiary, or the exclusion and restriction of occupation by other beneficiaries, is not exhaustive. The difficulty in practice is for the trustees to determine what is the equitable payment.

Under a trust for sale the law was uncertain whether one co-owner who had sole occupation could be ordered by the court to pay an occupation rent to the others who were not in occupation.

A person who is already in occupation whether because he is in occupation under the right to occupy provisions, or for some other reason, is protected. The trustees may not, in exercising their powers to exclude or restrict occupation, prevent a person either directly or indirectly from continuing in occupation unless that person consents or the court gives approval.

The court in deciding whether to give approval has to take into account the same matters as the trustees do in exercising their powers to exclude or restrict the beneficiaries occupation of the land (the intentions of the person who created the trust, the purpose for which the land is held and the circumstances and wishes of the beneficiaries who are, or would be, but for restriction or exclusion, entitled to occupy the land).

5. Advice. Section 6 of the Trustee Investment Act 1961 provides that a trustee must have regard to the need for diversification of investments and to their suitability. Apart from those investments in Part I of Schedule 1 to the Act, namely narrower-range investments which can be made without advice, a trustee must before investing under the Act obtain advice from a person the trustee believes to be qualified in financial matters, as to diversification and suitability. The advice must be given or confirmed in writing. If one of the trustees has the necessary competence there is no need for an outside adviser. Advice must also be obtained about retention of investments made under the Trustee Investment Act. "A trustee ... shall determine at what intervals the circumstances and in particular the nature of the investment, make it advisable to obtain such advice aforesaid, and shall consider such advice accordingly," section 6(3).

Maintaining equality

There is a general duty to maintain equality between the beneficiaries. "The trustees must act fairly in making investment decisions which may have different consequences for different classes of beneficiaries." (Hoffman J. in *Nestlé v. National Westminster Bank plc* (1988)).

1. The duty to convert. The trustees have a duty to maintain equality between the life-tenants and those entitled in remainder. They must make sure not only that the life-tenant receives an adequate income but that the capital is safe for the remainderman. Therefore, under the rule in *Howe v. Earl of Dartmouth* (1802) there is an implied duty to sell certain investments and reinvest the proceeds in authorised investments. The rule applies where the following criteria are fulfilled:

   (a) a residuary bequest—(it does not apply to a specific bequest) by will (it does not apply to intestacy);
   (b) of personal estate (the rule does not apply to real property);
   (c) to be enjoyed by persons in succession (the rule is directed towards preserving the trust property for beneficiaries with different interests); and
   (d) which consists of hazardous (unauthorised, speculative investments) wasting (those assets which will be short-lived, *e.g.* mineral rights, ships, cows, racehorses) or reversionary property, (those interests which are not yet vested in possession).

The wasting and hazardous securities are converted in the interest of the remainderman. They will often produce a high income but the capital is at risk. The reversionary interest is converted in the interest of the life-tenant for it will be producing no income.

The duty to convert can be expressly excluded in the will or by implication. The rule has been held not to apply where the testator expressly authorises the retention of unauthorised investments, or where he gives the trustees a power to sell when they see fit. If there is an express trust for sale, the rule will be excluded.

2. The duty to apportion. There may be a delay before the trustees convert the property. Subject to a contrary intention in the will, there are various rules governing the rights of the life-tenant and remainderman in the income.

(a) Authorised investments. The tenant for life is entitled to all the income. Authorised investments include those investments which although of a wasting or hazardous nature the testator has directed can be retained.

(b) Leaseholds. Where the land is settled leases over 60 years are authorised investments and so the rule in *Howe v. Earl of Dartmouth* does not apply. There is a duty to convert shorter leases but probably not a duty to apportion. Under a trust of land the life-tenant is entitled to all the income.

(c) Unauthorised personalty other than leaseholds. Where there is a duty to sell, whether express or implied, unauthorised investments, then pending sale there is an apportionment of income so that the life-tenant does not receive more or less than his fair share. If there is more income then the excess will go to capital; if less it can be made up out of the income from future years or from capital when it is realised.

The life-tenant is entitled to income based on the capital value. Where there is no power to postpone sale the value is ascertained at the end of one year from the testator's death. This is known as the executor's year and it is the time which is considered reasonable for an executor to wind up the deceased's estate. However, if the securities are actually sold during the year then the capital value will be the net proceeds of sale. Where there is a power to postpone sale, the value is taken at the testator's death, no other date being appropriate. In every trust of land, which may include personalty there will be a power to postpone the sale despite any provision to the contrary.

The life-tenant has in the past been entitled to an income of 4 per cent on the capital so valued. Today this is unrealistically low. Instead, the court may adopt the rate of interest equivalent to the court's short-term investment account, *Bartlett v. Barclays Bank Trust Co. Ltd (No. 2)* (1980).

(d) Reversionary interests. A reversionary interest produces no income. Therefore when it is sold or falls in, some of the capital should be paid to the life-tenant in compensation. The capital which the remainderman is entitled to is the amount which if invested at four per cent per annum (accumulating at compound interest at that rate with yearly rests and deducting income tax) would result in the total money actually received. The balance goes to the tenant for life. This is known as the rule in *Re Earl of Chesterfield's Trusts* (1883).

(e) Real property. There is no duty to apportion, even where there is an express direction to convert, real property. The tenant for life is entitled to the whole of the income.

The rules of apportionment are so complicated they are often excluded in the will. The exclusion of the duty to convert will necessarily exclude the duty to apportion but the testator could exclude the duty to apportion without excluding the duty to convert. Common will precedents exclude both conversion and apportionment.

Duty to avoid a conflict of interest

A trustee may not make a profit from his trust. He must not put himself in a position where his duty to the trust and his own personal interest may conflict.

1. The rule in *Keech v. Sandford* (1726). A trustee of a lease applied for its renewal for the benefit of an infant beneficiary. It was refused but the landlord agreed to renew the lease in the trustee's own favour. There was no question of fraud but it was held that the trustee held the lease on trust for the infant. The reason was that there would be less incentive on the trustee to press for a renewal for the trust if he knew that he would benefit by a refusal.

However, the rule applies only where the renewal is obtained by a trustee or some other person in a fiduciary position. Thus in *Re Biss, Biss v. Biss* (1903) where a yearly tenant of a shop died intestate and a renewal was refused to his widow, one of the children who subsequently obtained a renewal was held to be able to keep the lease for himself. There was no possibility at that stage that the lease would be renewed for the benefit of the estate nor did the child abuse his position in any way; he had no duty to the estate.

The freehold reversion is not part of the trust property and so the trustee ought to be able to buy the reversion for his own benefit unless he is directly depriving the trust. Thus if there is fraud, or if the lease is usually renewed and this could be jeopardised by the trustee purchasing the reversion, or if the trustee's position as lessee enabled him to buy the reversion there will be a conflict of interest and so the rule in *Keech v. Sandford* would apply. In other cases it should not. However, in *Prothero v. Prothero* (1968) the rule was held to apply whenever the trustee purchases the freehold.

2. Purchase of the trust estate. The purchase of trust property by a trustee, however fair the transaction, is voidable by any beneficiary. The rule is sometimes referred to as the self-dealing rule, *Tito v. Waddell (No. 2)* (1977). This rule applies even where there is a public auction, *Ex p. Lacey* (1802). It has been held not to apply to a bona fide sale either to a relative (but the closer the relative the more likely the sale is to be set aside), or to a company in which the trustee has shares (unless he is a majority shareholder or controls the company, *Farrars v. Farrars Ltd* (1888). If a trustee retires in order to purchase the trust property then any sale is voidable. Such an intention will be presumed if a sale follows closely after retirement. A sale was not set aside where the trustee had retired 12 years before he purchased the property, *Re Boles and British Land Co.'s Contract* (1902). Where a trustee obtains an option to purchase, the court is likely to set it aside as the trustee could exercise his option when prices are low. In *Wright v. Morgan* (1926) an option was set aside even though the price was fixed by an independent valuer. An option was upheld in *Re Mulholland's W.T.* (1949) where the option was granted to the bank by a testator before the bank took up the trusteeship on his death.

The trustee can purchase the trust property if expressly authorised to do so by the trust instrument or by the court. Section 68 of the Settled Land Act 1925 enables the tenant for life to purchase trust property.

The self-dealing rule has been held not to be confined to situations where the trustee was both vendor and purchaser (*Holder v. Holder* 1968) but applied also where a trustee concurred in a transaction which could not be carried into effect without his concurrence and the transferee was a company of which he was a managing director and in which his family had a majority shareholding, *Re Thompson's Settlement* (1986).

3. Purchase from the beneficiary of his beneficial interest.

In this case the trustee is not buying from himself and so there is an initial presumption of validity. This rule is sometimes referred to as the fair-dealing rule. In *Morse v. Royal* (1806) a middle-aged ex-army officer sold his interest to the trustee. There was no concealment or deceit by the trustee. When the property went up in price the beneficiary, who had pressed the trustee to buy the property, regretted the sale and sought to have it set aside. He failed. The position would have been different if there had been undue influence.

4. Remunerative employment.

A trustee must not use his position in order to obtain remunerative employment. Thus a stockbroker trustee had to hand over to the trust the commission he earned on valuation by his firm of the trust assets, *Williams v. Barton* (1927). Often a trustee will obtain remuneration as a director of a company. If he acquired his directorship because of his position as a trustee he will be accountable to the trust, *Re Macadam* (1946) but not if the trustees were directors before they became trustees, *Re Dover Coalfield Extension Ltd* (1908) or if the trustees were appointed directors without any reliance on the trust votes, *Re Gee* (1948). Often the will or settlement will authorise the trustee to keep the remuneration, *Re Llewellin's W.T.* (1949).

5. Agents, solicitors, company directors and others in a fiduciary position.

Similar principles apply to such people who are accountable for any profits they make because of their position. In *Boardman v. Phipps* (H.L., 1967) Boardman, a solicitor, administered a business in which the trust had an interest and made large profits both for the trust and himself. Although he had acted bona fide throughout, he was held accountable for his personal gains subject to a liberal allowance for his expertise and hard work. Boardman had only been able to make the profit because of the confidential information he had received while administering the trust.

6. Remuneration of the trustee.

One of the consequences of the rule that a trustee must not make a profit from his trust is that a trustee cannot charge for his time and trouble, *Barrett v. Hartley* (1866). Nor can a director of a company in the absence of a binding contract, *Guiness plc v. Saunders* (1990). Even a solicitor trustee cannot charge for anything other than his out-of-pocket expenses.

There are exceptions:

(a) If all the beneficiaries are *sui juris* and there is no possibility of undue influence they can agree to the trustee being paid.

(b) The court has a statutory jurisdiction to authorise payment where it appoints a corporation to be a trustee, section 42 of the Trustee Act 1925. A Judicial Trustee may be paid out of trust property, section 1(5) Judicial Trustees Act 1896. The court also has an inherent jurisdiction to allow a trustee to be paid where there is no charging clause in the trust instrument, or to vary or increase the amount where there is a charging clause. In *Re Duke of Norfolk's Settlement* (1981) a trust corporation accepted the administration of the trust for a low annual fee. As trustee, it subsequently became involved in an extensive redevelopment project in the Strand and was allowed an increase in remuneration because the duties became unexpectedly onerous.

(c) The Public Trustee can charge and so can a custodian trustee, Public Trustee Act 1906. A custodian trustee is either the Public Trustee or a corporation appointed to hold the documents and assets of the trust while the management, powers and discretion remain vested in the management trustees.

(d) Solicitor-trustees' costs of litigation. According to the rule in *Cradock v. Piper* (1850) a solicitor-trustee is entitled to profit costs in litigation where he acts as solicitor for himself and co-trustee in relation to the trust, provided the costs are not more than they would have been had he acted for the co-trustee alone. A solicitor-trustee cannot employ his firm to do non-litigious work but he could employ a co-partner in the unlikely event of the partner being exclusively entitled to the profit costs for his own benefit.

(e) The trust instrument may authorise the remuneration of the trustee. Many professional trustees would not undertake the trusteeship unless there were a charging clause, both to cover the professional services and the other trustee duties which a layman could undertake. In *Re Gee* (1948) there was an express provision for the solicitor-trustee to charge for "work done by him in the administration of the trust." The court held that he was entitled to charge only for the work which required his professional skills.

7. Reimbursement. A trustee is entitled to be reimbursed out-of-pocket expenses such as insurance premiums and money spent on repairs. Section 30(2) of the Trustee Act 1925 provides "A trustee may reimburse himself or pay or discharge out of the trust premises all expenses incurred in or about the execution of the trusts or powers." A trustee will be allowed his litigation costs if the court grants leave to sue or defend. In other cases the trustee will obtain costs only if the action was properly brought or defended for the benefit of the trust estate, *Holding & Management Ltd v. Property Holding & Investment Trusts plc* (1990).

8. Competitive business. If the trust contains a business as part of its assets then the trustee should not compete. In *Re Thompson* (1930) the trust property included a yacht broker's business, a very specialised trade. A trustee wanted to set up a similar business in the same locality. The court issued an injunction restraining the trustee for his firm would have taken trade away from the trust.

Duty to keep accounts and provide information

Trustees must keep clear and accurate accounts and produce them to any beneficiary when required. A beneficiary is entitled to all reasonable information about the administration of the trust. When a beneficiary reaches 18 he should be informed of his interest under the trust. Beneficiaries are entitled to see all trust documents and title deeds, *O'Rourke v. Darbishire* (H.L., 1920). Trustees are not, however, bound to give reasons why they have exercised their discretion in a particular way, and so are not bound to disclose documents, such as trust minutes, which contain this confidential information, *Re Londonderry's Settlement* (1965). A disgruntled beneficiary could bring proceedings alleging bad faith, and then the documents would be available on discovery.

Section 22(4) of the Trustee Act 1925 gives the trustees an absolute discretion to have the accounts audited but no more than once in every three years unless there are special circumstances.

---

14. POWERS

In the exercise of a power the trustees must be unanimous unless there is a provision in the trust instrument to the contrary.

Various powers have been conferred on trustees by statute including the power to sell, partition and insure the trust property, see Parts I and II of the Trustee Act 1925. Trustees of land have, for the purpose of exercising their functions as trustees, all the powers of an absolute owner, section 6(1) of the Trusts of Land and Appointment of Trustees Act 1996.

This chapter will deal with three powers, maintenance, advancement and delegation.

MAINTENANCE

Express power

The trust instrument may give the trustees a discretionary *power* to apply income for the maintenance and education of children, or there may be an express *trust* to do so. If it is a power the trustees must honestly decide whether to exercise their power and if they do so the court will not interfere; but trustees cannot delegate to someone else a discretionary power which is given to them personally, *Re Greenslade* (1915), nor can they give the whole fund to a parent without exercising their discretion at all, *Wilson v. Turner* (1883).

Statutory power

The statutory power of maintenance is found in section 31 of the Trustee Act 1925.

(a) Before the beneficiary reaches 18 the trustees may, subject to contrary intention, section 69(2), pay to his parent or guardian, or otherwise apply, the whole or part of the income of the property for his maintenance, benefit or education.

(b) After 18, if the beneficiary still has not a vested interest, then the trustees must pay the whole of the income to the beneficiary, unless there is a direction to the contrary. In *Re McGeorge* (1963) the testator devised certain land to his daughter, the gift not to take effect until after the wife's death. The 21-year-old daughter claimed the income. The court held that she was not entitled to maintenance from the income because the gift was deferred which indicated a contrary intention.

(c) Vested interest. Usually there will be income available where the interest is vested, unless the beneficiary is entitled to a share of the income only under a discretionary trust, or there is a prior life interest.

(d) Contingent interest. In a contingent interest the beneficiary will be entitled to income only if the property which is the subject-matter of the trust carries the intermediate income.

All testamentary gifts carry the intermediate income, unless it is otherwise disposed of, except for deferred residuary gifts and contingent pecuniary legacies, L.P.A. 1925, s.175. In three special cases contingent pecuniary legacies will carry the intermediate income:

(1) Where the legacy was given to a minor by his father or some person *in loco parentis*, the contingency is reaching 18, and there is no other fund available for maintenance, Trustee Act 1925, s. 31(3).

(2) Where the testator has shown an intention that the beneficiary should be maintained. The testatrix in *Re Churchill* (1909) gave a pecuniary legacy to her great-nephew. She directed her trustees to pay money towards the advancement of him in life "or otherwise for his benefit." The court held it carried the intermediate income and so maintenance was available.

(3) Where the testator sets aside a special fund for the legatee but makes it contingent. For example a gift of £10,000 to Bella at 18.

(e) Gifts to classes. Where property is given to a class contingently on attaining 18 the vesting of one person's share does not prevent the trustees from applying the income from the presumptive shares of the others for their maintenance.

(f) Accumulation. If there is an express direction to accumulate income until a certain age this may indicate that the testator does not want the statutory power of maintenance to apply. Thus in *Re Erskine's S.T.* (1971) a direction that the income be accumulated indicated that there should be no maintenance even though the direction was void for perpetuity.

Section 31(2) provides that all the income arising during infancy which is not disturbed should be accumulated and invested. If necessary the trustees can apply the accumulations for the benefit of any infant beneficiary as if they were income from the current year. The beneficiary is entitled to the accumulations on reaching his majority (or earlier marriage) if either he is then entitled to the capital or during his minority he had a vested interest in the income, section 31(2).

(g) The making of maintenance payments is in the sole discretion of the trustees whether or not there is "any other fund applicable to the same purpose; or . . . any person bound by law to provide for his maintenance or education." The payments must be reasonable and the trustees should consider the age of the minor, his requirements and all the circumstances of the case including what other income is available.

The court's power

The court has an inherent jurisdiction to allow a minor's property to be used for his maintenance. Usually the court will only apply income for maintenance, ignoring where necessary a direction to accumulate, but it also can use capital. The court also has a statutory power to sell a minor's property to provide funds for his maintenance, section 53 of the Trustee Act 1925.

ADVANCEMENT

Express power

An express power to apply capital (as distinct from income as in maintenance) for the advancement or benefit of a minor or contingent beneficiary is sometimes given in a trust instrument. Advancement means making some permanent provision for a beneficiary, *e.g.* buying a house for him to set up as medical practitioner, *Re Williams W.T.* (1953). Benefit has a wider meaning and would include paying the beneficiary's debts.

In *Re Clores S.T.* (1966), as part of a tax-saving scheme and in order to fulfil the moral obligations of the wealthy beneficiary, capital was applied by making donations to charities. It was considered to be for the benefit of the beneficiary.

Whatever the terms of the power the trustees must exercise their discretion in making the advance and make sure that the purpose of the advance is really carried out. In *Re Pauling's S.T.* (1964) the trustees, charmed by the life tenant's husband, advanced to the children capital sums from their presumptive share. Although nominally for the benefit of the children, the capital was really used to maintain the luxurious lifestyle of their parents. Subsequently the children succeeded in suing the trustees for breach of trust in making improper advances.

Statutory power

Unless there is a contrary intention every post-1925 trust has a statutory power to pay capital for the advancement or benefit of any person entitled to the capital, or any share thereof, even if there is a possibility that the beneficiary's interest may be defeated. Although the section is restricted to trust property which is personalty, where the beneficiary wanted to buy trust land, it was held that rather than give him the money so that he could buy the land, the property could be conveyed direct, *Re Collard's W.T.* (1961). Besides being limited to personal property the other limitations of the statutory power of advancement are:

(a) the capital advanced must not exceed half the beneficiary's vested or presumptive share;

(b) when the beneficiary's interest vests, any advances must be brought into account in calculating his share; and

(c) the advance must not prejudice the prior life, or other, interest of any person (*e.g.* a life-tenant) unless he is *sui juris* and gives his written consent.

The trustees can apply the money "in such manner as they may, in their absolute discretion, think fit." Benefit, as in express powers of advancement, is given a wide meaning. "It means any use of the money which will improve the material situation of the beneficiary," *per* Viscount Radcliffe in *Pilkington v. Inland Revenue Commissioners* (H.L., 1964). In *Pilkington* the trustees suggested in order to save tax that an advance be made to a young beneficiary and that the advance should be resettled on new trusts. It was held that such an exercise was within the statutory power (though in the case it was void for perpetuity) and that it did not matter that incidentally the family of the beneficiary might benefit.

Court's power

Under section 53 of the Trustee Act 1925 the court has power to make an order authorising an infant's property to be transferred so that the capital or income can be applied for the maintenance, education or benefit of the infant.

DELEGATION

The general rule is that a trustee cannot delegate his trust powers for he has been selected for his personal qualities and wisdom.

However, trustees have always been able to delegate where special skills are required. A stockbroker could be employed to buy and sell shares, a solicitor to do conveyancing. Trustees would be liable if they did not select the proper man for the job and supervise his activities.

The position is now governed by section 23(1) of the Trustee Act 1925:

"Trustees or personal representatives may, instead of acting personally, employ and pay an agent, whether a solicitor, banker, stockbroker or other person to transact any business or do any act required to be transacted or done in the execution of the trust, or the administration of the testator's or intestate's estate, including the receipt and payment of money, and shall be entitled to be allowed and paid all charges and expenses so incurred, and shall not be responsible for the default of any such agent if employed in good faith."

This section has changed the law in that the trustees no longer have to show a special need for expertise before they can delegate.

What is less clear is whether the trustees, having made an appointment in good faith, are liable if they fail to supervise the agent so appointed.

In *Re Vickery* (1931) the defendant employed a solicitor to wind up a small estate. The beneficiaries objected to the solicitor's appointment. Subsequently they disclosed to the defendant that the solicitor had been suspended from practice. The defendant allowed small sums of money to be received and held by the solicitor who later absconded with the money. The plaintiffs failed in their action for a declaration that the defendant had been guilty of a breach of trust. Maugham J. relied on sections 23(1) and 30 of the Trustee Act.

Section 23(1) exempts the trustee from *vicarious* liability for the action of agents. It is not inconsistent with this to hold a trustee *personally* liable for failing to supervise.

In *Re Lucking's Will Trust* (1968) Lucking was a shareholder beneficiary and sole trustee in a trust fund which consisted of a majority holding in a company. His friend Dewar was appointed by the company as managing director. Lucking signed blank cheques which Dewar countersigned and then used the money for his own purposes. On Dewar's bankruptcy £18,000 was irrecoverable and Lucking was held liable for breach of trust. He had not acted as a prudent man of business, *Speight v. Gaunt* (1883). Section 30 did not apply as the trust property was not deposited with Dewar.

Section 30 imposes personal liability on a trustee for acts of others who have received trust property only if the trustees' own wilful default has allowed the breach to occur. Wilful default for the purposes of section 30 was limited by Maugham J. to conscious wrongdoing. This part of the case has been heavily criticised, see Chapter 16.

Section 23(2) gives trustees wide powers to delegate where the trust property is outside the United Kingdom. Section 23(3) provides that trustees may appoint solicitors and bankers to receive trust moneys, but the trustees will be liable if they permit the property to remain in control of the solicitor or banker for longer than is necessary.

Under section 25 of the Trustee Act 1925, as amended by section 9 of the Powers of Attorney Act 1971, the trustee can by power of attorney delegate all his trustee duties and powers to an agent for a period not exceeding 12 months. Notice has to be given to the other trustees and to any person having power to appoint a new trustee, although failure to do so does not invalidate any act of the agent. A trustee cannot delegate to a co-trustee unless such a trustee is a trust corporation. If the agent defaults the trustee is liable as if the failure were his own.

Section 9 of the Trusts of Land and Appointment of Trustees Act 1996 enables trustees to delegate their functions, including the power of sale, to beneficiaries of full age beneficially entitled with an interest in possession to the trust land. The delegation must be by power of attorney,

A third party dealing in good faith with the donee of a power can presume, unless the third party had at the time of the transaction actual knowledge to the contrary, that the donee is the beneficiary to whom the functions could be delegated.

A subsequent purchaser can rely on a statutory declaration made by a third party before or within three months of the completion of the sale to the effect that he dealt in good faith and did not have such knowledge.

A power of attorney must be given by all the trustees but may be revoked by any one of them. If a new trustee is appointed then the power will automatically be revoked. However, where there is no new appointment the death or retirement of a trustee will not cause the power of appointment to lapse.

The general rule is that if the functions are delegated to a beneficiary and he ceases to be entitled to an interest in possession in the land subject to the trust the power is revoked. If the functions are delegated to him and other beneficiaries jointly and each of the beneficiaries ceases to be entitled to an interest then the power is revoked. However, if only one or some of the beneficiaries cease to be entitled, the functions continue to be exercisable by the remaining beneficiaries. If the functions are delegated to him separately, or separately and jointly, the power is revoked as far as he is concerned.

A delegation may be made for any period of time or indefinitely. However, the power of attorney cannot be an enduring power of attorney under the Enduring Powers of Attorney Act 1985.

The trustees' liability is limited. Although they are liable both jointly and severally for any default of a beneficiary in exercising the functions this liability arises only if the trustees did not exercise reasonable care in deciding to delegate.

Beneficiaries, to whom the functions have been delegated have the same duties and liablities as the trustees. For these purposes only they are in the same position as trustees. They are not, however, regarded as trustees for any other purpose. They cannot sub-delegate their functions nor can they receive capital monies so as to overreach the equitable interest of any beneficiary.

15. VARIATION FROM THE TERMS OF THE TRUST

SAUNDERS v. VAUTIER (1841)

A trustee must carry out the trust according to the terms of the trust instrument and the rules of equity. For trusts created or arising after the commencement of the Trusts of Land and Appointment of Trustees Act 1996, trustees are bound to consult the benficiaries, of full age and beneficially entitled to an interest in possession in the land and so far as is consistent with the general interest of the trust, to give effect to their wishes. The trust instrument may exclude the need to consult.

Under the rule in *Saunders v. Vautier* (1841) beneficiaries who are *sui juris* and together entitled to the whole beneficial interest can terminate the trust and demand that the trust property be handed over to them. And where there is a direction to accumulate income exclusively for the benefit of one beneficiary he can on reaching his majority terminate the accumulation and demand the property.

VARIATION BY THE COURT

Generally the court has no power to authorise a departure from the terms of the trust. In the words of Farwell J. in *Re Walker* (1901) "I decline to accept any suggestion that the court has an inherent jurisdiction to alter a man's will because he thinks it beneficial. It seems to me that is quite impossible." There are situations, however, where the court will intervene either under its inherent jurisdiction or where there is statutory provision.

Inherent jurisdiction

1. Salvage and emergency. The court has an inherent power to authorise a departure from the terms of a trust where an unforeseen emergency arises or for the purposes of salvage. An example of salvage would be doing repairs to prevent a building from collapsing, *Re Jackson* (1882). The power is limited to management and administration. It does not extend to variations of beneficial interests.

2. Compromise. The court has a limited jurisdiction to approve compromises on behalf of minors and unascertained beneficiaries. "Compromises" have been given a restricted interpretation. There has to be an element of dispute and not a mere family arrangement in which a beneficiary gives up a present right in return for a different right, *Chapman v. Chapman* (H.L., 1954). In *Mason v. Farbrother* (1983) trustees of a pension fund applied to the court to give them wider powers of investment than under the Trustee Investment Act 1961. There was a dispute concerning the original investment clause but the court refused to substitute a new investment clause under its inherent jurisdiction. Instead the variation was permitted under section 57 of the Trustee Act 1925.

Statutory provisions

1. Section 57(1) of the Trustee Act 1925. This section, like the inherent jurisdiction, permits variation of a trust for purposes of administration and management. The court can intervene where it is expedient to do so even where there is no emergency. Section 57 gives no power to vary the beneficial interests under a trust, *Re Downshire S.E.* (1953). The provisions of the section are deemed to be incorporated into every settlement. The section has been used to authorise the sale of chattels, the sale of land where the necessary consents were refused, the purchase of a residence for the tenant for life and to give wider investment powers.

2. Section 64(1) of the Settled Land Act 1925. This section gives the court power to sanction departures from the trust which are for the benefit of the land or the beneficiaries provided they could have been effected by an absolute owner. The section is not limited to management and administration and can be used to alter beneficial interests. Before the Variation of Trusts Act 1958 it was often used to minimise tax.

3. Section 53 of the Trustee Act 1925. Under this section the court can authorise dealings with an infant's property for his maintenance, education or benefit. There has always been a more limited inherent jurisdiction for this purpose.

4. The Variation of Trusts Act 1958. This Act was passed because of the decision in *Chapman v. Chapman* (1954) when the House of Lords refused to vary the beneficial interests of a trust under the court's inherent jurisdiction to compromise claims.

Under the Act variations can be made covering not only administrative matters but also beneficial interests, provided the arrangement is for the benefit of the person on whose behalf the court is giving approval. The Act has been used for a variety of purposes, including inserting a power of advancement, terminating an accumulation and inserting an accumulation period, but it is most often used for saving tax.

(1) Persons on whose behalf the court may approve an arrangement

According to section 1(1) of the Variation of Trusts Act 1958:

"Where property, whether real or personal, is held on trusts arising, whether before or after the passing of this Act, under any will, settlement or other disposition, the court may if it thinks fit by order approve [any arrangement] on behalf of—

(a) any person having, directly or indirectly, an interest, whether vested or contingent, under the trusts who by reason of infancy or other incapacity is incapable of assenting; or

(b) any person (whether ascertained or not) who may become entitled directly or indirectly, to an interest under the trusts as being at a future date or on the happening of a future event a person of any specified description or a member of any specified class of persons, so however that this paragraph shall not include any person who would be of that description, or a member of that class, as the case may be, if the said date had fallen or the said event had happened at the date of the application to the court; or

(c) any person unborn; or

(d) any person in respect of any discretionary interest of his under protective trusts where the interest of the principal beneficiary has not failed or determined."

An illustration of the proviso in (b) occurred in *Re Suffert* (1951). Income was given on protective trusts to a woman for life and on her death, subject to a general testamentary power, to those entitled under the rules of intestacy. She had three adult cousins who were entitled. One cousin was made a party and consented. The court refused to consent on behalf of the other two who were not before the court.

The same reasoning prevented the court approving a variation for adult beneficiaries in *Knocker v. Youle* (1986). Another reason for the failure of the application was that the cousins had an interest, albeit remote and contingent, so that they could not be described as persons "who may become entitled . . . to an interest under a trust."

(2) The meaning of benefit

Benefit does not mean just solely financial benefit, though variations have usually been made to save tax. In *Re Weston's Settlements* (1969) Lord Denning said "The court should not consider merely the financial benefit to the infant and unborn children but also their educational and social benefit. There are many things in life more worthwhile than money." In *Re Remnant's S.T.* (1970) the removal of a forfeiture provision on practising Roman Catholicism was a benefit for its retention could cause trouble within the family. It has also been held that it would benefit a mentally handicapped person to give away his property if that is what he would have done had he been of sound mind, *Re C.L.* (1969).

The benefit does not have to be a certainty if there is a reasonable chance that it will occur. Thus arrangements have been made which depend on a woman having no more children or a life-tenant dying before a particular date, *Re Cohen's Settlement* (1976). In the case of paragraph (d) the court can approve an arrangement that is not for the benefit of those entitled under the discretionary trust.

(3) Effect of the order

The Act does no more than give the court power to consent to arrangements on behalf of those unable to consent themselves. Adult ascertained beneficiaries have to give their own consents. The legal result is that the variation of the trust is effected not by the court but by the consent of the parties, *Re Holt's Settlement* (1969).

Nevertheless the variation takes effect as soon as the order is made by the court without any further instrument being needed for the purposes of section 53(1)(c) of the L.P.A. 1925, *Re Hambleden's W.T.* (1960).

The old trusts are replaced by new trusts with the result that the perpetuity period begins afresh, *Re Holt's Settlement* (1969).

5. Matrimonial Causes Act 1973.   The court has wide powers to make orders concerning the allocation of property between the parties in matrimonial proceedings. These powers include varying ante- and post-nuptial settlements for the benefit of the parties to the marriage and their children.

6. Mental Health Act 1983.   The Court of Protection has power under this Act to make a settlement of a patient's property and to vary such settlement should there be any substantial change in circumstances.

16. BREACH OF TRUST

A trustee is liable for acts of omission, failing to do what he ought to do, and acts of commission, doing what he should not do. Some breaches may be only minor and may in fact be beneficial to the trust. The trustee will not be liable in such circumstances if the court would have authorised the transaction.

A beneficiary has four remedies against the trustee for a breach or a threatened breach of trust.

INJUNCTION

A beneficiary may seek an injunction to restrain a breach of trust. For instance, an injunction might be obtained to prevent the grant of an unauthorised mortgage.

PERSONAL REMEDY AGAINST THE TRUSTEES

If the trustee commits a breach of trust then he is liable to account to the trust estate for the loss. If he is in breach of duty in failing to act then he is liable to account for what he would have received but for his wilful default. Wilful default in this context includes not only conscious wrongdoing but also a mere failure to carry out his duty as a prudent trustee, *Bartlett v. Barclays Bank Trust Co. Ltd* (1980).

Personal not vicarious liability

1. A trustee is liable for his own acts and defaults and not for those of others. Section 30(1) of the Trustee Act 1925 provides:

> "A trustee shall be chargeable only for the money and securities actually received by him notwithstanding his signing of any receipt for the sake of conformity, and shall be answerable and accountable only for his own acts, receipts, neglects, or defaults and not for those of any other trustee,

nor for any banker, broker or other person with whom any trust money or securities may be deposited, nor for the insufficiency or deficiency of any securities, nor for any other loss, unless the same happens through his own wilful default."

A trustee will thus be liable for his co-trustee only where he is himself at fault. Examples are:

(a) leaving trust income in the hands of a co-trustee for too long without making proper inquiries, *Townley v. Sherborne* (1634) or allowing one trustee to receive capital;

(b) concealing a breach committed by his fellow trustees, *Boardman v. Mossman* (1779); and

(c) standing by while to his knowledge a breach of trust is being committed, *Booth v. Booth* (1838) or contemplated, *Wilkins v. Hogg* (1861).

"Any other loss" has to be construed *eiusdem generis* and is limited to the situations covered by the section. According to Maugham J. in *Re Vickery* (1931), applying the words of Romer J. in the company case of *Re City & Equitable Fire Insurance Co. Ltd* (1925), a trustee will not be guilty of wilful default under this section "unless he knows that he is committing and intends to commit a breach of duty, or is recklessly careless in the sense of not caring whether his act or omission is or is not a breach of his duty." This interpretation has been criticised. In other cases of breach of trust wilful default does not necessarily involve conscious wrongdoing. It also includes failure to act as a prudent man of business, *Speight v. Gaunt* (1883).

2. Breaches by former and subsequent trustees. A trustee is not liable for breaches of trust committed by his predecessors. He should, however, sort out any irregularities he discovers when taking office including obtaining satisfaction from the old trustees. Generally a trustee is not liable for breaches committed by his successors unless he retired so that the breach could be committed. Mere recognition that his retirement would facilitate a breach is not sufficient, *Head v. Gould* (1896).

Measure of liability

1. Capital liability. (a) Losses. Unauthorised investments. Where a trustee makes an unauthorised investment he is liable for the loss incurred when it is sold, *Knott v. Cottee* (1852). Where he wrongfully retains an unauthorised investment he is liable for the difference between the price he obtains when it is sold and the price which he would have obtained had he sold it at the right time. In *Fry v. Fry* (1859) the unauthorised investment was an inn. An offer was made for it in 1837 which was refused as being inadequate. In 1859 the inn was sold for a much lower price due to a falling off of trade following the building of a railway. The trustees were held liable for the difference in price.

Authorised investments. Where too much money is advanced on an authorised investment the trustee is liable for the excess, section 9 of the Trustee Act 1925. Where a trustee improperly realises an authorised investment he must replace it or pay the difference between the price obtained and the cost of repurchasing the investment, *Phillipson v. Gatty* (1848). Where the court has to assess the cost of replacing the investment, it will be valued at the date of judgment, *Re Bell's Indenture* (1980).

(b) Profits. If a profit arises from a breach of trust the beneficiaries can claim it, *Daker v. Somes* (1834). A trustee cannot claim that a profit made in one transaction should be set off against a loss suffered in another unauthorised transaction. In *Dimes v. Scott* (1828) the trustee retained an unauthorised investment and paid all the income to the tenant for life. When the investment was realised, due to a fall in the investment market, the trustees were able to purchase more consols than they would have been able to had they purchased them at the proper time. The trustees were held liable for the excess interest they had paid to the tenant for life and were not allowed to set off the gain they had made by paying for the consols at a lower price. If, however, there are not two distinct transactions but the gain and loss are part of the same transaction, then the rule against set-off will not apply. In *Fletcher v. Green* (1864) money was invested in an unauthorised mortgage. The security was sold at a loss, the proceeds paid into court and invested in consols which rose in price. The trustees were held able to take advantage of the price rise as it was part of the same transaction. A modern case where this was followed is *Bartlett v. Barclays Bank Trust Co. Ltd* (1980), where the bank was able to set off the losses on a development project at the Old Bailey against the profits made on another development at Guildford, both resulting from a policy of unauthorised speculative investments.

2. Interest.   As well as repaying the capital the trustee is liable to pay interest to the trust fund where the loss results from an unauthorised investment or payment of the trust estate to the wrong person. He must also pay interest where he is guilty of undue delay in investing the trust funds.

The rate of interest is in the discretion of the court. It used to be fixed at 4 per cent except where:

(a) the trustees actually received more than 4 per cent when they would be liable for the full amount they did receive;

(b) the trustees ought to have received more. For instance, where they realised a proper investment producing a high rate of interest they would be charged with the interest they would have received had they retained the investment;

(c) the trustees were presumed to have received more as where the trustees traded with the money. The beneficiary could claim either 5 per cent or the actual profits made by the trustees;

(d) the trustees were guilty of fraud or serious misconduct in which case the court might charge them with 5 per cent compound interest.

Today the court realises that these low interest rates are unrealistic. In *Wallersteiner v. Moir (No. 2)* (1975) the trustee was charged compound interest at 1 per cent above the minimum lending rate where he was held to have traded with the funds and in *Bartlett v. Barclays Bank Trust Co. Ltd* (1980) the bank was liable to pay interest at the rate prevailing on money in the court's short-term investment account.

Impounding trustee's beneficial interest

Any beneficial interest a trustee has can be withheld to make good his breach of trust, *Re Dacre* (1916).

Joint and several liability

Trustees are liable jointly and severally. Any one of the trustees may be sued for the full amount or, if they all are sued, judgment may be executed against any one (or more) of them.

Before 1978 all trustees who were in breach were liable equally and so if one had paid more than his share he could claim a contribution from the others. Under the Civil (Liability) Contribution Act 1978 the court has a wide discretion to fix the amount of contribution from a co-trustee depending on what is fair and reasonable in all the circumstances.

In some cases it may be appropriate for a trustee to be completely indemnified rather than to bear a share of the loss with the other trustees. Indemnity was possible as an alternative to equal contribution before the 1978 Act and was awarded in exceptional circumstances. Examples were where:

(a) one trustee acted fraudulently or was alone morally culpable, *Bahin v. Hughes* (1886);

(b) the breach was committed solely on the advice of a solicitor co-trustee, *Head v. Gould* (1898);

(c) only one trustee benefited from the breach; and where

(d) one of the trustees had a beneficial interest; this was used first to make good the loss before there was any contribution from the others, *Chillingworth v. Chambers* (1896).

Under the Limitation Act 1980 the trustees have two years within which to claim contribution. Time runs either from the date of judgment against a trustee for breach of trust or from the date when the trustee compromises the beneficiary's claim.

If a trustee overpays a beneficiary the trustee can adjust the accounts by making deductions from future income, *Liversey v. Liversey* (1827). But if he underpays himself and overpays others then he cannot adjust the accounts if this would cause hardship to the beneficiaries.

Protection of trustees

The trust instrument may restrict or extend the liability of a trustee but where a breach of trust does occur there are several instances where a trustee may escape liability.

1. Relief by the court. Under section 57 of the Trustee Act 1925 a trustee may apply to the court for authorisation to effect a dealing with the trust property not permitted by the trust instrument. If a breach has already been committed, the court may relieve a trustee from liability if he "acted honestly and reasonably, and ought fairly to be excused for the breach of trust and for omitting to obtain the directions of the court in the matter in which he committed such breach," section 61 of the Trustee Act 1925.

In *Re Kay* (1897) the testator left £22,000. The apparent liabilities of the estate were £100. The trustee advertised for creditors of the estate, having previously given the widow £300. It turned out that the testator's debts amounted to more than £22,000. The court held that the trustee had acted honestly and reasonably. It was unforeseeable that the actual debts would be more than £22,000 when the apparent debts were £100.

Obtaining legal advice before acting may not be sufficient to bring the trustee within section 61. In *National Trustees Co. of Australasia Ltd v. General Finance Co. of Australasia Ltd* (1905) the trustees followed the advice of a solicitor which was incorrect. The trust was

large and complicated and the court held that the advice of a trust
expert, a senior counsel, should have been sought.

There are no rules when relief will be granted under section
61. The courts have insisted that each case be judged on its own
particular circumstances but the burden lies on the trustee to
establish that he acted reasonably and honestly and as prudently
as he would have done in organising his own affairs. "A paid
trustee is expected to exercise a higher standard of diligence
and knowledge than an unpaid trustee," *per* Harman J. in *Re
Waterman's W.T.* (1952).

2. Acts of beneficiaries. (a) Pre-breach. If a beneficiary, who
is of full mental capacity, not under the influence of his parents,
and *sui juris*, concurred in or participated in any breach then he
cannot proceed against a trustee. For a full discussion of this principle see *Re Paulings S.T. (No. 1)* (1964).

(b) Post-breach. A beneficiary *sui juris* and with full knowledge
of the facts may by release or subsequent confirmation preclude
himself from taking proceedings against a trustee for breach of
trust.

(c) Indemnity. The court has an inherent jurisdiction to order
that a trustee be indemnified out of the interest of a beneficiary
who instigated such a breach. If the beneficiary merely concurred
in the breach then it must be shown he received a benefit from it.

Section 62 enlarges the court's power. It provides: "Where a
trustee commits a breach of trust at the instigation or request or
with the consent in writing of a beneficiary, the court may, if it
thinks fit ... make such order as to the court seems just, for
impounding all or any part of the interest of the beneficiary in the
trust estate by way of indemnity to the trustee or persons claiming
through him."

3. Discharge in bankruptcy. The effect of the Insolvency Act
1986 is that where a bankrupt trustee has obtained his discharge
then he will be freed from further liability except where he was a
party to a fraudulent breach of trust.

4. Limitation Act 1980. The normal rule is that an action
for breach of trust must be brought within six years of either
(1) the breach of trust, or (2) the beneficiary's interest vesting
in possession or (3) the beneficiary obtaining his majority, which-
ever is the latest.

No period of limitation applies to an action by a beneficiary, "in respect of any fraud or fraudulent breach of trust to which the trustee was a party or privy" or "to recover from the trustee the trust property or the proceeds thereof in the possession of the trustee or previously received by the trustee and converted to his use." However the doctrine of laches may apply.

A trustee, who is also a beneficiary, is, after the limitation period, only liable to replace the excess over his proper share. This relief is available only where he acted reasonably in making the distribution, *Re Somerset* (1894).

The limitation period does not apply to a claim by the Attorney-General against the trustee of a charitable trust which has no "beneficiary," *Att.-Gen. v. Cocke* (1988).

TRACING

Tracing involves getting the actual property back, or the asset which represents it. If property gets into the hands of B, A can in certain circumstances trace the property and reclaim it from B.

Tracing has several advantages over a mere personal claim:

(a) It may be available where there is no effective personal claim as where the trustee is insolvent and the person who has the property is an innocent volunteer.

(b) If the person (B) who has the property goes bankrupt then the owner (A) can claim priority over B's creditors. A is a secured creditor as he has a proprietary claim which is attached to the property.

(c) Claimants are entitled to any income produced by the assets which have been traced from the date on which the property came into the defendant's hands. Claims *in personam* only carry interest from the date of judgment.

(d) In some cases the plaintiff will not just be entitled to the return of his money but also to any increase in the value of the property.

Following at common law

At common law following the property was possible as long as it was not mixed with other property. Thus identifiable tangible property could be followed, or a *chose in action* (*e.g.* a bank balance) or property purchased with the plaintiff's money.

In *Taylor v. Plummer* (1815) the defendant handed money to his stockbroker to purchase exchequer bonds. The stockbroker purchased American investments instead. On the stockbroker's bankruptcy the defendant was entitled to the investments which represented the money he had given to the stockbroker.

However, once money is mixed, as in a bank account, there can be no following at common law.

Another limitation of common law was that it did not recognise equitable rights. A beneficiary under a trust could not at law follow his property into the hands of the trustees.

Tracing in equity

Tracing in equity is possible where:

(a) there is an equity to trace;

(b) the property is traceable; and

(c) the tracing does not produce an inequitable result.

1. There must be an equity to trace. In order for the remedy to be available there must be some initial fiduciary relationship. It is not sufficient merely to show that the defendant has been unjustly enriched.

In *Lister v. Stubbs* (1890) the defendant was the plaintiff's agent. He received secret commissions. Part of this money he invested in land. The plaintiff was unable to follow the money because there was not a fiduciary relationship, only a contractual one, between the principal and agent. This case was followed in *Re Att.-Gen's Reference (No. 1)* (1985) where a publican made a secret profit by selling his own beer in breach of his contract with the brewer. However *Lister v. Stubbs* was disapproved by the House of Lords in *Att.-Gen for Hong Kong v. Reid and others* (1993). A solicitor acting for the Hong Kong Government received bribes. He was held liable to account for the bribes and for the increased value of the property representing the bribes.

The most obvious example of a fiduciary relationship is between a trustee and a beneficiary but sometimes the contract itself will give rise to a fiduciary relationship.

In *Aluminium Industrie Vaasen B.V. v. Romalpa Aluminium Ltd* (1976) the plaintiff company sold aluminium foil to Romalpa. A term of the contract was that ownership in the aluminium would pass to Romalpa only when Romalpa completed payment. On the liquidation of Romalpa, before payment to the plaintiff had been completed, the plaintiff company was held entitled to trace money in Romalpa's account which represented the proceeds of sale of the foil to sub-purchasers. Since *Romalpa* the courts have been reluctant to uphold fiduciary relationships of this kind. See *Tatung (U.K.) Ltd v. Galex Telesure Ltd* (1989). A retention clause will only operate so as to give the seller of goods an interest in any proceeds of subsale if registered as a security charge under the Companies Act 1985.

An extreme example of the court finding a fiduciary relationship is *Chase Manhattan Bank N.A. v. Israel British Bank (London) Ltd* (1981). The Chase Manhattan Bank paid money to another bank by mistake. That bank paid the money to the Israel British Bank, which then went into liquidation. It was held that the Chase Manhattan Bank had a continuing equitable proprietary right in the money which enabled it to trace and acquire priority over the general creditors. The mistaken payment to the defendant itself gave rise to the fiduciary relationship. See also *Westdeutsche Landesbank Girozentrale v. Islington B.C.* (1993) (tracing available where contract void because *ultra vires*).

In *Agip (Africa) Ltd v. Jackson* (1989) Millet J. said "The requirement [that there must be some fidicuary relationship] is, . . . readily satisfied in most cases of commercial fraud, since the embezzlement of a company's funds almost inevitably involves a breach of fiduciary duty on the part of one of the company's employees or agents."

2. The property must be traceable. It may be easy to trace money as where it has been invested in shares. In this case the beneficiary can claim either the property itself or a charge on it for the money expended in the purchase, *Sinclair v. Brougham* (1914). It is sometimes impossible to trace as where the money has been dissipated on living expenses. The difficulty arises where money has been mixed and the separate funds cannot be identified. There are various rules for dealing with the problem.

(a) The onus is on the trustee to establish what is trust property and what is his own. If he cannot do this then the whole will be treated as trust property, *Lupton v. White* (1808).

(b) If a trustee mixes the funds of two trusts or an innocent volunteer mixes his own funds and that of a trust in an unbroken bank account the rule in *Clayton's Case* (1816) may be applied. The first payment out is set against the first payment in and vice versa; "first in first out" unless there is an express appropriation. The rule can be excluded expressly by agreement or by implication from the circumstances. See *Barlow Clowes International v. Vaughan* (1992).

(c) Where a trustee mixes trust funds with his own the rule in *Re Hallet's Estate* (1880) may be applied. A trustee is presumed to draw on his own money first before using the trust money. He is not expected to want to commit a breach of trust. It is only when his own money is exhausted that he is taken to be drawing trust funds. For example: Trustee has £1,000 in an account, £500 of his own funds, £500 of trust funds. He then spends £500 on a holiday. The £500 is deemed to be his own money even if it was credited to the bank account after the trust funds. *Re Hallet* thus has displaced the rule in *Clayton's Case*.

(d) Where a trustee draws out more than his own money and is therefore spending some of the trust funds any money of his own he subsequently pays in will not, without express appropriation, go to restoring the trust funds. To continue with the example given in (c) above, if the trustee dissipates a further £400 and later pays in £200 of his own the beneficiaries cannot claim this amount. They can claim only the lowest intermediate balance, namely £100, *Roscoe (James) (Bolton) Ltd v. Winder*.

(e) *Re Hallet* is subject to the overriding principle that the beneficiary has a first charge on any property bought out of a mixed fund. In *Re Oatway* (1903) a trustee withdrew money from a mixed fund and invested it. Later he withdrew the rest of the money which he dissipated. In such circumstances the creditors could not claim that the trustee was deemed to spend his own money first so that they were entitled to the investments. The beneficiaries claim had to be satisfied out of any identifiable part of the mixed fund before the trustee, or his creditors, could make any valid claim. Thus the beneficiaries were entitled to the investments.

(f) Any trust money paid into the trustee's bank account to reduce the trustee's overdraft must be repaid. The debt will be charged on any properties purchased with the help of the overdraft but the beneficiaries will not be able to claim any part of the properties themselves. The reason being that the money is used to repay the debt, not to purchase the property, *Re Tilley's W.T.* (1967).

(g) In cases other than bank accounts where a trustee mixes funds of different trusts, (or a volunteer mixes his own money with trust funds) and identification is not possible then the beneficiaries under the respective trusts, (or the beneficiary and the volunteer) will have a charge on any property bought with the mixed funds. They will share the charge rateably (*pari passu*).

In *Sinclair v. Brougham* (1914) a Building Society ran an *ultra vires* banking business. When the society was wound up the depositors succeeded in establishing a fiduciary relationship between them and the directors. They were held entitled to trace funds in the hands of the society *pari passu* with the shareholders.

(h) If an innocent volunteer mixes his own money with trust money and the property increases in value then the increase will be shared rateably. A *fortiori* a beneficiary should be entitled to a proportion of the increase where a trustee mixes funds of his own with trust funds. According to Jessel M.R. in *Hallet* and Lord Parker in *Sinclair v. Brougham* a beneficiary is entitled only to a charge on the property. However, in *Re Tilley's W.T.* Ungoed-Thomas J. stated *obiter* that a beneficiary should be entitled to an increase. This must be correct otherwise a trustee would be profiting from his breach of trust.

3. The tracing must not produce an inequitable result

(a) A right to trace cannot be exercised against a bona fide purchaser for value without notice of the equity.

(b) No claimant can trace who has acquiesced in the wrongful mixing or distribution.

(c) No tracing will be allowed where it would cause injustice. If an innocent volunteer improves his own house with the use of trust moneys then tracing will not be allowed, for it would result in the sale of the house. If he had bought a house, however, partly with trust money, tracing will be allowed for both he and the beneficiaries can be restored to their original positions by the repayment of money.

Most of the principles of tracing are illustrated in *Re Diplock* (1948). By his will Diplock gave his residuary estate to "such charitable institutions or other charitable or benevolent objects as my executors may in their absolute discretion select." The executors, thinking this was a valid charitable gift, distributed £203,000 amongst various charities. The next-of-kin succeeded in their claim to trace against the charities by establishing a fiduciary relationship between themselves and the executors. There was held to be nothing inequitable in tracing property into the hands of innocent charitable institutions. It was, however, considered to be impracticable to trace funds which had been spent on improving part of a building in the middle of a hospital. Where the charities held the funds without mixing with other funds then all the money was held for the next-of-kin. Where the money had been mixed the charity and the next-of-kin shared *pari passu*.

PERSONAL REMEDY AGAINST RECIPIENT

If tracing is not available, as where the funds have been dissipated, it may be possible for the beneficiaries to pursue a personal remedy against the person who wrongfully received the property. This remedy is available where there has been overpayment in administering an estate but it may not be available in the case of other trusts, *Re Diplock* (1948).

---

17. SAMPLE QUESTIONS AND MODEL ANSWERS

Question 1

Gladstone and Bower are trustees of a trust of land which they hold for the benefit of Zoe and Foster as tenants in common. Part of the land consists of a farmhouse which Zoe wants to occupy. Gladstone has no objection to this, but Bower does. Zoe would like to have Bower removed as a trustee. She would also like to control the trust property and not have to rely on the trustees.

Advise Zoe.

Answer

The issues raised in this question relate to a beneficiary's right of occupation, the power of a beneficiary to remove a trustee and the delegation of a trustee's powers.

1. The right of occupation. Section 12(1)—The Trusts of Land and Appointment of Trustees Act 1996 provides:

> "A beneficiary who is beneficially entitled to an interest in possession in land subject to a trust of land is entitled by reason of his interest to occupy the land at any time if at that time—
> (a) The purposes of the trust include making the land available for his occupation (or for the occupation of beneficiaries of the class of which he is a member or of beneficiaries in general) or
> (b) The land is held by the trustees so as to be so available."

Zoe would appear to be entitled to an interest in possession, having a present right of present enjoyment, and so prima facie is entitled to occupy the land. However, the rights conferred by the section set out above do not apply if the land is either unavailable or unsuitable. If the farmhouse is part of a working farm and Zoe has no farming experience, she will have no automatic right of occupation.

Moreover, Foster also is entitled to an interest in possession. The trustees could decide that he should be given the right to occupy the property. Under section 13 the trustees can restrict or exclude the right of occupation where two or more beneficiaries are entitled. They can also impose reasonable conditions, including the payment of outgoings and compensation. In exercising the power to exclude or restrict occupation, the trustees have to consider, amongst other things, the intentions of the person who created the trust, the purposes for which the land is held and the circumstances and wishes of each of the beneficiaries who is entitled to occupy the land.

2. Directions for the removal of a trustee.   Where there is no person nominated for the purpose of appointing new trustees by the trust instrument and the beneficiaries under the trust are of full age and capacity and together are absolutely entitled to the property subject to the trust, beneficiaries may give a direction for the retirement or appointment of a trustee. In this case as there are only two trustees, if directions are going to be given for the retirement of Bower, then another trustee would have to be appointed.

However, in order to give an effective direction, the beneficiaries must be unanimous. If Foster is happy with Bower as a trustee and does not want to join in with the direction, then Zoe will not be able to insist on the retirement of Bower.

3. Delegation.   Under section 9 of the Trusts of Land and Appointment of Trustees Act 1996, Trustees are given wide powers to delegate to any beneficiary or beneficiaries of full age beneficially entitled to an interest in possession in the trust property any of their functions as trustees which relate to the land. A delegation is by Power of Attorney. The delegation could be given to Zoe alone, rather than to both the beneficiaries. However, the delegation must be made by all the trustees. It appears unlikely from the facts that Bower would agree to such a delegation.

Although once the delegation has taken place the trustees are not liable for any default of the beneficiary, they can be liable if they do not exercise reasonable care in deciding to delegate the function in the first place. As part of the general law, trustees are under a duty to hold the balance between the beneficiaries. It appears from the facts that Zoe is making the demands and the trustees before delegating should make sure that the interests of Foster are properly protected.

Even if the power of sale were delegated to Zoe any capital money would have to be paid to the trustees and not to her personally.

Question 2

Advise the organisation known as Feminists For Freedom (FFF) on whether its charter's aims entitled it to charitable status.

(1) The FFF seeks to promote a greater understanding of feminist literature, to which end it seeks to publish works by female authors, including books dealing with prostitution. The FFF also seeks to establish a feminist-oriented library for FFF staff and their families.

(2) The FFF seeks to provide accommodation for female single parents on 60-year non-assignable leases at below market price for those who would otherwise be homeless and therefore in need. The FFF does not seek to make a profit from the provision of accommodation and any surplus funds will be used to provide creche facilities for the single mothers.

(3) The FFF seeks, through lobbying and peaceful demonstration, to change the law relating to gender discrimination and equal pay in this country and abroad and thereby alleviate the lot of all women and improve their life in general.

(4) The FFF seeks to assist the campaign to allow the ordination of women in the Roman Catholic Church in the belief that this will increase the size of congregations.

(5) The FFF seeks to advance the study by girls and women at schools and institutions of further and higher education in engineering, law, computer sciences, physics and other studies usually associated with men.

What difficulties, if any, will there be in the event that only some of the clauses are deemed charitable?

Answer

In order for the FFF to achieve charitable status it must show that its objects are exclusively charitable and have a sufficient element of public benefit. There is not a legal definition of what is a charitable purpose but the courts pay attention to the charitable objects specified in the Charitable Uses Act 1601 even though this Act has now been repealed. These purposes have been summarised by Lord Macnaghten in *Commissioners of Income Tax v. Pemsel* (1891) as trusts for (1) relief of poverty (2) advancement of religion (3) advancement of education (4) other purposes beneficial to the community which do not fall under any of the other heads.

Clause (1)

This clause could constitute a trust for the advancement of education. Education is not confined to the classroom (*Re Hopkins*

(1965)). Pornography as such would not be educational in this sense (*Re Pinion* (1965)). It is unlikely that books published by feminists would be pornographic. They are more likely to have a serious social purpose. The library although educational would not be charitable as it is restricted to FFF staff and their families. It would therefore not be of general public benefit (*Oppenheim v. Tobacco Securities Trust Co. Ltd* (1951)). As the library is not an ancillary purpose the whole clause would fail. There is no legislation in this country as there is in Australia and New Zealand to strike out the non-charitable elements.

Clause (2)

There can be no effective charitable trust under the heading of poverty if the gift could benefit the rich as well as the poor (*Re Gwyon* (1931)). Single female parents are not necessarily poor but the facts of the question do state that "they would otherwise be homeless and therefore in need." In *Joseph Rowntree Memorial Trust Housing Association Ltd v. Att.-Gen.* (1983) it was held that the fact that the accommodation was provided by way of bargain on a contractual basis rather than by way of bounty did not prevent the trust from being charitable. Nor did it matter that the length of the leases might outlast the needs of the beneficiaries as they might well do on the facts of the question. The position would be different if FFF intended to profit from the arrangement and not to use such profit for charitable purposes.

Clause (3)

Prima facie this would come under the fourth charitable head, namely a trust for purposes beneficial to the community. However changing the law is a political purpose and political purposes are not charitable (*McGovern v. Att.-Gen.* (1982)). This rule applies where the aim is to change the law or government policy at home or abroad.

Clause (4)

It could be argued that this creates a trust for the advancement of religion. Larger congregations mean more people going out into the world to "mix with their fellow citizens" (*Neville Estates Ltd v. Madden* (1962)). On the other hand there would need to be a change in canon law to allow women priests and this aim might therefore fail, being tainted with a political purpose.

Clause (5)

This would succeed as a trust for education being for the benefit of a sufficiently large section of the community. It does not matter that the trust is for women only. Section 43 of the Sex Discrimination Act 1975 provides that the Act does not apply to any provision in a charitable trust conferring benefits on one sex only.

If any one of the clauses is non-charitable then FFF would not acquire charitable status (*Oxford Group v. I.R.C.* (1949)). It would be otherwise if a fully charitable purpose incidentally conferred a benefit on objects which are not charitable (*Re Coxen* (1948)). FFF should redraft clause 2 so that the library is available to the public at large and delete clauses 3 and 4. The taxation advantages would make this exercise worthwhile.

Question 3

Buster leaves all his property to his wife "secure in the knowledge that upon her death anything she has that came from me she will leave to such of my relatives and such of those persons she knows to be my old friends as she should think fit."

Discuss whether this establishes a valid trust.

Answer

In order to create a valid trust the three certainties must be established; certainty of intention, subject-matter and objects (*Knight v. Knight* (1840)).

It is possible on the wording that Buster did not intend to impose a trust on his widow but merely to express a hope that she might deal with the property in a certain way (*Re Adams & The Kingston Vestry* (1884)). It is not necessary that he should have used the word trust but the words must be strong enough to impose an obligation on her. The fact that Buster did not leave his widow a mere life interest in the property or restrict her dealing with it in any way suggests an absolute gift. On the other hand construing the will as a whole may lead to the conclusion that he intended a trust.

The subject-matter of the trust is clear in that Buster left his entire estate to his wife, not using vague words like "the bulk of my estate" (*Palmer v. Simmonds* (1854)). However it is not clear what is the size of the beneficial interests. It may be that the wife should have only a life interest (*Re Last* (1958)). In such a case though entitled to the income she would not be entitled to the capital. In *Sprange v. Barnard* (1789) where a testatrix left her property to her husband Sprange for his sole use and "at his death the remaining part of what is left, that he does not want for his own wants and uses," to be left to others, the court held Sprange was absolutely entitled to the property on the ground that "the property and the person to whom it is to be given must be certain in order to raise a trust." Another possibility is that there might be a floating trust as in *Ottaway v. Norman* (1972) which would crystallise only on the death of the widow. During her lifetime she could deal with the property as an absolute owner but on her death she would have to leave it according to Buster's directions. On the wording of this particular trust the widow would be under a fiduciary duty not to dispose of the assets of the trust, or a substantial part of them, so as to defeat the interests of the friends and relatives.

The trust for the friends and relatives is a discretionary trust so there is no need for a complete list of beneficiaries (*Mcphail v. Doulton* (1971)). It must however be possible to say of any given person that he is or is not a relative or friend. Taking relatives to mean next-of-kin (*per* Stamp L.J. in *Re Baden* (1973)) the class is conceptually certain but old friends is too vague. In *Re Barlow's Will Trusts* (1979) Browne-Wilkinson J. gave some guidelines on friends. He said:

"(a) the relationship must have been a long-standing one; (b) the relationship must have been a social relationship as opposed to a business or professional relationship; (c) although there may have been long periods when circumstances prevented the testatrix and the applicant from meeting, when circumstances did permit they must have met frequently."

He was however dealing with gifts subject to a condition precedent where it seems the rules as to certainty of objects are less stringent. Moreover in this case there is a further difficulty in that the friends have to be old friends. This would mean that the class would be conceptually uncertain were it not for the provision that the widow is to decide who were the testator's old friends. It is permissible for a third party to determine who should be within the class (*Re Tuck S.T.* (1976), questions of Jewish blood and faith should be determined by the chief rabbi).

Taking the whole clause together it appears that the testator did not wish to restrict his widow's use of the property during her life and was happy to rely on her judgment for its disposal on her death. The tenor of the clause is not to create a trust but to give her an absolute gift on the assumption that she would want on her death to leave the property to his friends and relatives.

Question 4

On November 29, Martin told Jill that if she agreed, he hoped that she would, at some future date, act as his trustee, holding on behalf of Nathan. On December 1, Martin made his will leaving his home, Dunborin, and £100,000 to Jill "on such trusts as I have indicated to her" and the residue of his estate to Hanbury. On December 2 Martin handed Jill a sealed envelope saying that the contents confirmed their conversation of November 29 but that it was only to be opened upon his death.

Three years later in April Jill told Nathan that when Martin died he would be a very wealthy person. In July in the same year Nathan became a vegetarian and immediately declared himself trustee of any interests in property he would receive upon Martin's death, for the benefit of the National Vegetarian Council, a registered charity.

Nathan died on October 1, choking on a raw carrot. Martin did not know of this before his very recent death last month.

Advise Jill, Nathan's estate and the National Vegetarian Council. The letter, when opened, stated that Dunborin and the £100,000 were to be held on trust for Nathan.

Answer

Martin's will leaves his home Dunborin and £100,000 to Jill as trustee. There is thus no possibility of Jill taking the property beneficially. Jill will either hold the property on trust for Nathan, if a half-secret trust can be established, or if not for Hanbury, who is entitled to Martin's residuary estate.

Before a half-secret trust will be valid it must be established:

(1) That there has been a sufficient communication of the terms of the trust *before* or *at the same time as* the will. The rule is based on unsatisfactory dicta in *Blackwell v. Blackwell* (H.L., 1929) and has been severely criticised. In fully secret trusts where the trustee appears to take beneficially on the face of the will, communication can take place at any time before the testator's death. There is no logical reason why this rule should not be the same for half-secret trusts.

(2) There must be acceptance of the terms by the trustee.

(3) There must be no conflict between the terms of the will and the secret trust.

It is impossible to tell from the facts whether there was a sufficient communication on November 29. To be effective Jill must have been told of the property to be comprised in the trust (*Re Colin Cooper* (1939)). If not the subsequent letter will not be a sufficient communication. Although communication can take place in a sealed envelope, provided the trustee knows it contains the terms of the trust (*Re Keen* (1939)), in this case it will be ineffective as the letter is given a day after the will. It could be argued that this is *de minimis* and is effectively contemporaneous with the will. If all the terms were communicated on November 29 then the letter will satisfy L.P.A. 1925, s.53(1)(*b*) which stipulates that trust of land must be evidenced (*i.e.* not made) in writing.

Jill can accept the trust by implication. It appears that there is no conflict between the will and the terms of the trust which are alleged to have been communicated on November 29. If however, the real communication is by letter contemporaneous with the will then there is a conflict, for the trusts had not at that stage been communicated. Thus Nathan could not claim the property.

Nathan has purported to declare a gift of his expectancy under Martin's will. According to *Re Ellenborough* (1903) a declaration of non-existent property is void. However, if there is a valid half-secret trust in his favour, he may be able to establish that he had an interest in the property from the date of the communication of the trust to Jill. This follows from another unsatisfactory case *Re Gardner (No. 2)* (1923), where a gift to a beneficiary was held not to lapse even though the beneficiary died before the testator (though after the communication of the trust to the trustee). Even if it is accepted that secret and half-secret trusts operate *dehors* the will, it is difficult to understand how the trust could be properly constituted before the death of the testator. Nathan can declare a trust orally of the £100,000 but the declaration respecting Dunborin would have to be evidenced in writing to satisfy the L.P.A. 1925, s.53(1)(b). It might also be argued that the declaration was in fact a disposition of an equitable interest which needs to be made, not merely evidenced, in writing and this section would apply not only to the house but also to the money. In *Grainge v. Wilberforce* (1889) it was said that where there is a sub-trust, the original beneficiary will disappear from the picture and the property will be held by the original trustee direct for the beneficiary of the sub-trust. It appears from the facts given that Nathan had no active duties to perform as a trustee so it might indeed be held to be a disposition.

The parties should therefore be advised that it is possible that there was no valid half-secret trust so that Jill should hold the property for Hanbury. However even if there were a valid trust for Nathan it is highly unlikely, due to the nature of Nathan's interest and the lack of formalities, that the National Vegetarian Council could claim the property. It is most likely that Nathan's estate would benefit.

Question 5

Tom is a trustee of property for his nephew Nick who is 10. The trust property consisted of £50,000 in cash, some Government securities, and some valuable antiques.

Tom gave the £50,000 to his daughter Bella. She had no knowledge of the trust. She used the money to buy a house which she redecorated. She has just resold the house for £70,000.

Tom has sold the antiques to a bona fide purchaser for value without notice of the trust and spent the proceeds on a holiday in Greece.

The income from the Government securities was credited to Tom's bank account. He opened the account in May this year, which shows the following transactions. Credits May 2: £400 (income from Nick's trust), May 4: £200 (income from another trust), May 6: £100 (money Tom won on a horse), June 10: £200 (further horse winnings). Debits May 10:£100 money withdrawn, May 15, a further £100 withdrawn.

Advise Nick's mother.

Answer

As a trustee, Tom is under a duty to conserve the trust assets. If he is in breach of trust, the beneficiary can sue him for the loss to the trust estate. Where Tom has insufficient assets of his own, or where the property has increased in value, it will be in the interests of the beneficiary to recover the actual trust funds or the property into which they have been converted.

Nick cannot follow the property according to the common-law rules as he has only an equitable interest under a trust. (Even if he had a legal interest he could not follow his property into a mixed fund.) He can, however, trace the property in equity if three conditions are fulfilled. First there has to be an initial fiduciary relationship. This condition is fulfilled as there is a trust. Tom is holding the property on behalf of his nephew Nick. Secondly the property must be traceable, and thirdly tracing must not produce an inequitable result. It is necessary to consider these two conditions when dealing with the separate items.

As Bella was not aware that the money was trust money and as she did not give any consideration she is an innocent volunteer. This means she is not liable as a constructive trustee but it is not considered inequitable to trace the trust funds in her hands. Nick is entitled to the £70,000 representing the original £50,000 and the increase in its value. If, however, Bella had spent substantial sums on the property she would be entitled to share *pari passu* (rateably) in the increase in value as well as reclaiming her initial expenditure (*Re Diplock* (1948)).

It is not equitable to trace against a bona fide purchaser for value who has no notice of the trust. The proceeds, having been spent, are irrevocable. The property no longer exists and so cannot be traced (*Re Diplock* (1948)).

Money deposited in bank accounts is traceable according to special rules. Where a trustee mixes trust money with his own he is presumed to pay out his own money first rather than to have committed a breach of trust (*Re Hallet's Estate* (1880)). Thus the £100 paid out on May 10 would be taken to be the £100 he paid in on May 6 as a result of his horse-winnings. When he made the second withdrawal on May 15 he no longer had any money of his own in the account. Nor would the payment in on June 10 be taken to replace the trust moneys unless that was Tom's specific intention (*Roscoe v. Winder* (1915)). Tom therefore has withdrawn £100 of trust money. Though it might be fairer that the loss should be borne by the two trust funds rateably this is not the law. The rule in *Clayton's Case* (1816), first in, first out, will be applied. In other words the withdrawal is deemed to be made from the £400 representing the interest on Nick's funds. The rule, which originated as a rule of commercial convenience, results in Nick's trust bearing the whole of the loss while the other funds remain intact.

Nick's mother should be advised that Nick will be entitled to trace the £70,000 and the £300 in the bank account. A personal action could be brought against Tom for the dissipation of the other moneys. She should also be advised to apply for Tom to be removed from the trust under the court's inherent jurisdiction.

Question 6(a)

Chive told Garlic that he wanted her to hold some shares in a private company on trust for Marjoram and Thyme. He then telephoned the director of the company asking him to carry out the details of the transfer.

The next day Chive was involved in an accident at his home. Marjoram and Thyme visited him. He told them of his conversation with Garlic and handed the share certificates to them. Unexpectedly, Chive died that night from his injuries. Garlic is the executor of Chive's will.

Advise Marjoram and Thyme.

Question 6(b)

Parsley covenanted with Dill and Mint that he would transfer Cabbage-Patch to them to hold on trust for his co-habitee, Rosemary, and their child Basil. His will, made earlier, had left all his property to Sage.

At his death Cabbage-Patch had not been transferred.

Advise Rosemary.

Answer (a)

In order to be enforceable a trust must be properly constituted either by the settlor making a declaration of trust or by transferring the trust property to trustees. A trust of shares can be declared orally but an ineffective transfer will not be construed as a declaration (*Jones v. Lock* (1865)).

Chive has purported to transfer the shares to Garlic. He has not done so effectively. As Turner L.J. said in *Milroy v. Lord* (1862) "there is no equity ... to perfect an imperfect gift." To transfer shares a share transfer form must be executed and the shares registered by the company in the name of the transferee. If, however, the transferor has done everything he needs to do, for example executing the transfer, but the effectiveness of the gift depends on a third party the gift will not fail (*Re Rose* (1952)). Where the transferor needs to take some further steps, like obtaining Treasury consent, the gift will not be effective (*Re Fry* (1946)). On the facts Chive has merely made a telephone call which is clearly not sufficient.

Where a donor makes a gift in contemplation of imminent death, a *donatio mortis causa*, equity may in some circumstances perfect what would otherwise be an imperfect gift. The gift must have been made in contemplation of imminent death (*Duffield v. Elwes* (1827)). Here Chive died but he did not make the gift because he expected to die for his immediate death was unanticipated.

Another difficulty for Marjoram and Thyme if they want to enforce the gift is that only certain property is capable of being the subject-matter of a *donatio mortis causa*. It may be that shares cannot be (see *Ward v. Turner* (1752)) and *Re Weston* (1902) but contrast *Staniland v. Willott* (1852)). Even accepting that shares are capable of being the subject-matter of a *donatio mortis causa*, the handing over of the share certificates without a completed form of transfer would probably not amount to sufficient delivery of the gift.

Marjoram and Thyme may be more successful under an extension of the rule in *Strong v. Bird* (1874). Where there is a continuing intention by the donor to make a gift and the property has been lawfully vested in the donee in another capacity, as where he is the personal representative of the deceased, the gift will be effective. In this case, however, Garlic is not the intended beneficiary but only the trustee. Nevertheless in *Re Ralli's Will Trust* (1964) this principle was extended to a situation where a trustee obtained the legal estate in another capacity, namely as sole surviving trustee under a will. Thus Garlic will be bound to hold the shares for Marjoram and Thyme. This is of course a quite fortuitous result as Chive might easily have appointed someone other than Garlic as executor.

Answer (b)

This is another example of an incompletely constituted trust. Parsley has not transferred the subject-matter of the trust to the trustees but has merely covenanted to do so.

Incompletely constituted trusts cannot be enforced by volunteers. Rosemary and Basil gave no consideration and there is no question of marriage consideration for Rosemary and Parsley are not married nor is there any evidence of a settlement made in contemplation of marriage.

There is of course a contract between Parsley and the trustees. The trustees could sue for breach of contract but as they have not lost anything their damages may be purely nominal. Moreover the court in *Re Pryce* (1917) refused to authorise the trustees to sue and in *Re Kay's Settlement* (1939) and *Re Cook's Settlement* (1965) the trustees were directed not to sue. The only case to the contrary is *Re Cavendish-Browne's Settlement* (1916) where trustees did sue for damages and succeeded. The damages were a sum equivalent to the value of the property comprised in the covenant and it was held that the money received by way of damages should be held on the trusts of the settlement. The case concerned specific land in Canada and so it could be argued that it could apply to Cabbage-Patch which is specific existing property.

There is no question of Dill and Mint obtaining specific performance as they did not give any consideration.

Rosemary and Basil might allege that there was a properly constituted trust of a *chose in action*, namely the benefit of the covenant to settle the property. This was found to be the case in *Fletcher v. Fletcher* (1844) but it is unlikely today that the facts would support the intention to create a trust of the covenant.

Rosemary should be advised that she has not a strong case for claiming Cabbage-Patch. If she does not succeed the property will pass to Sage under Parsley's will.

Question 7

In 1977 Baker purchased two adjoining plots of land: Homeacre, costing £10,000, and Backacre, costing £8,000. Baker told his solicitor that he wanted Homeacre conveyed "into the care of" his son, Lewis, and this was done. Lewis then built a house on Homeacre at a cost of £15,000 and, upon its completion in 1978, Baker said that Lewis could take over Backacre as a part of the garden. In reliance upon this, Lewis constructed a swimming pool in Backacre at a cost of £2,000.

In 1980 Baker executed a will by which, after appointing Lewis as his sole executor, he specifically devised Backacre to Charles and left all his residuary estate to Gertrude. Baker died earlier this year.

Advise Lewis, as executor, who is entitled to Homeacre and Backacre.

Answer

As an executor Lewis has a fiduciary duty towards all the persons entitled to his father's estate. He would be in breach of that duty if he simply claimed Homeacre and Backacre as his own. As regards Homeacre he obtained the legal estate by the conveyance in 1977, but it may be that he held the property on a resulting trust for his father. He has had the beneficial use of Backacre since 1978 but not the legal title.

Homeacre

Where property is conveyed into the name of one person, the purchase money being provided by another, there is a presumption that the legal owner will hold the property on a resulting trust for the person who provided the money (*Dyer v. Dyer* (1788)). Thus it might be that Lewis is holding the property on a resulting trust for Baker. Support is given to the presumption by the instruction given by Baker to his solicitor that he wanted the property conveyed "into the care of" his son Lewis. On the other hand there is another presumption, the presumption of advancement, which arises where the person providing the money is under an equitable obligation to support the person to whom the property is conveyed. So if the person who provides the money is the husband or father or stands *in loco parentis* to the person to whom the legal estate is conveyed then it will be presumed that a gift was intended. This presumption in turn can be rebutted as where the son is a solicitor or the parents are elderly and are not minded to deal with their own affairs (*Garrett v. Wilkinson* (1848)).

In this case it seems likely that a gift was intended by Baker to his son Lewis. Lewis presumably thought so otherwise he would not have spent money building a house on the property. Even if there was not an immediate gift in 1977 he has acted to his detriment in the expectation of acquiring some interest in the property and so should be entitled under the principle of proprietary estoppel (*Inwards v. Baker* (1965)). Though the court has a wide discretion in the remedies it can give for such an interest the most appropriate would seem to confirm that Lewis has a fee simple absolute (*Pascoe v. Turner* (1979)).

Further evidence that a gift was intended is found in the will itself. Baker makes no specific devise of Homeacre. The reason, no doubt, is that he considered he had already disposed of Homeacre in 1977.

Backacre

Backacre has been left to Charles. This might indicate that Baker did not intend to make a gift of the property to Lewis in 1978. The legal estate remained with Baker till his death. If there was a continuing intention by Baker to make a gift to Lewis then the appointment of Lewis as executor might perfect an imperfect gift under the rule in *Strong v. Bird* (1874). As executor Lewis will have the legal estate vested in him. The fact that Baker stood by while Lewis constructed a swimming pool might be evidence of a continuing intention to make a gift. If not Lewis might be able to claim an interest under the principles of proprietary estoppel as explained in relation to Homeacre. However, considering the relative value of the property and the cost of the swimming pool, which does not necessarily enhance the value of the property, the court might consider it appropriate merely to give Lewis a charge on the property for £2,000.

Lewis should be advised that he has a good claim to Homeacre but that it is unlikely that he will be entitled to Backacre.

Question 8(a)

The Oxford Young Methodists Association (an unincorporated body) decided to launch an appeal to provide funds to further its youth work "amongst youngsters who are, or are likely to become, Methodists in the Oxford area." Money is raised through collecting boxes, discos and raffles, in part, and by requiring the parents of those youngsters using its present facilities to pay 50p each week on behalf of their child(ren).

The association was recently overjoyed to receive on trust a legacy from Don of £1,000,000 "to be used to build facilities for the Oxford Young Methodists Association to use in their work, especially youth clubs."

Advise the association as to whether Don's gift will be a valid trust for a purpose.

Question 8(b)

During the building projects the Oxford Young Methodists Association is subsumed into the South East Region Young Methodists Association. Having met all its liabilities, the Oxford Association's bank account has a surplus of £100,000 which the Crown claims as *bona vacantia*.

Advise the members of the Oxford Association, all of whom were parents of the children using its facilities.

Answer (a)

Trusts normally must have a human beneficiary. Purposes trusts, with a few exceptions, are invalid unless they are charitable. It could be argued that this is a charitable trust under the fourth head given by Lord Macnaghten in *Pemsel's Case* (1891), being a trust for purposes beneficial to the community. The Recreational Charities Act 1958 provides that the provision of facilities for recreation and leisure-time occupation in the interests of social welfare can be charitable. Facilities needed for youth are specifically covered. However a trust must still be for the public benefit. Here the money is for an association which provides for only a small section of society, a class within a class, namely Methodists in the Oxford area. It would therefore fail (*Re Baddeley* (1955). This part of the decision is not affected by the Recreational Charities Act 1958.

A non-charitable purpose trust is prima facie void (*Leahy v. Att.-Gen.* (1959)). One of the reasons for this is that there is no one to enforce the trust. However, where property was given to trustees for the provision of a sports ground for employees, it was considered that the employees had a sufficient interest to be able to enforce the trust (*Re Denley* (1969)). Here the "youngsters" or their parents would have a sufficient interest to enforce the trust. Another problem with purpose trusts is that the capital can be tied up for ever, and thus offend the rule against inalienability. This problem was avoided in *Re Recher* (1972) by holding that the gift was intended to be an accretion to the funds of the society, which were subject to the members' control. They could therefore divide the capital among themselves at any time. In this case Don has specifically stated that he wants the money to be used for building facilities. In a similar case, *Re Lipinski* (1976), where money was given to the Hull Judean (Maccabi) Association for the construction of buildings the court was able to hold that the gift was nevertheless for the members of the association.

Provided that the members of the Oxford Young Methodists Association control the funds or can change their constitution so that they can do so (*cf. Re Grant's W.T.* 1980 where the constitution precluded such control and the constitution could not be altered without the approval of an outside body) then Don's gift will be a valid trust for the members of the association.

Answer (b)

Where an unincorporated association is dissolved there is often a problem about surplus funds. The South Eastern Region Young Methodists Association cannot claim the money unless the constitution of the Oxford Association provides for the money to be used for the purposes of any similar association.

There are three other possible claimants to the surplus funds; those who provided the money, the Crown, and the members of the association.

Where property is given on trust for a purpose which is no longer feasible or is surplus to requirements there is sometimes held to be a resulting trust in favour of those providing the money. In *Re Gillingham Bus Disaster Fund* (1959) money was collected for the victims of a road accident. Much more money was collected than was necessary. It was held that each donor had an interest under a resulting trust. This is clearly inconvenient where it is impossible to trace the donors. On the facts of the question there would be no difficulty about Don's legacy which could be held on a resulting trust for his estate (*Re West Sussex* (1930)) but there would be problems about money received from the general public through collecting boxes and discos.

A more practical solution is to regard money raised in such a way as an outright gift. Indeed where money is paid for raffles and discos those who pay have received what they contracted for (*Re*

West Sussex (1930)). Thus on the dissolution of the association the property no longer has an owner and would go to the Crown as *bona vacantia*.

The modern approach is to distribute the assets of an association on dissolution among its existing members (*Re Bucks. Constabulary Fund* (No. 2) (1979)). Although the case did not involve a legacy, the dicta by Walton J. in *Re Recher* (1972) is wide enough to preclude a resulting trust whatever the source of the money. So in the absence of rules to the contrary the surplus funds might be distributed to the members of the Oxford Association at the time of its dissolution. Any parents who have ceased to be members would not be entitled to claim (*Re Sick and Funeral Society of St. John's Sunday School, Golcar* (1973)). On the other hand Don's estate might claim the legacy on the basis of a resulting trust, relying on the recent case of *Davis v. Richards & Wallington Industries Ltd* (1991).

In any event the members of the association should be advised to contest the claim of the Crown.

INDEX